WRITING YOUR COLLEGE APPLICATION ESSAY

Writing Your College Application Essay

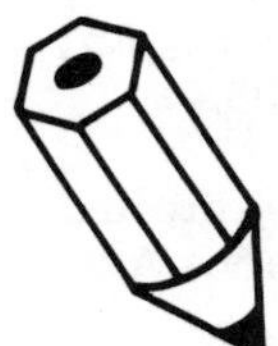

Sarah Myers McGinty

College Entrance Examination Board
New York

In all of its book publishing activities the College Board endeavors to present the works of authors who are well qualified to write with authority on the subject at hand and to present accurate and timely information. However, the opinions, interpretations, and conclusions of the authors are their own and do not necessarily represent those of the College Board; nothing contained herein should be assumed to represent an official position of the College Board or any of its members.

Copies of this book are available from your local bookseller or may be ordered from College Board Publications, Box 886, New York, New York 10101. The price is $9.95.

Editorial inquiries concerning this book should be directed to Editorial Office, The College Board, 45 Columbus Avenue, New York, New York 10023–6917.

Grateful acknowledgment is made for permission to quote as follows: on pages 47 and 57 from *The American Novel and Its Tradition* by Richard Chase, published by Doubleday & Company, Inc.; on page 63 from *The Poetry of Robert Frost* edited by Edward Connery Lathem. Copyright 1923, ©1969 by Holt, Rinehart and Winston. Copyright 1951 by Robert Frost. Reprinted by permission of Henry Holt and Company.

Interior design by Anne Scatto/Levavi & Levavi.

Library of Congress Catalog Number: 86–070268
ISBN: 0–87447–257–1

Printed in the United States of America

9 8 7 6 5 4 3 2 1

For Pete's sake

Contents

Acknowledgments

For anyone who has studied and taught English, writing a book is a wonderfully humbling experience. There is, of course, what Matthew Arnold called "the best that is known and thought in the world," the entire history of British and American literature, with which to compare one's effort. And then there are all the teachers, colleagues, officemates, and mentors (including my eleventh-grade English teacher, a history teacher whose classes are said to embody the charm and wit of a good cocktail party, and a marathon vice-principal) who have preceded me, shared with me, and inspired me. And last there are the best teachers in the world, 20 years of high school students. Writing this book meant continual collision with something learned from someone else. I acknowledge and thank all these sources, especially my students, and most particularly those Millburn High School students in the class of 1975 and in the class of 1986. Of all who have passed through room 210, it was the one in the front of the class who learned the most and had the most fun!

I also want to thank those who have guided this book to publication, Carolyn Trager, first and foremost, and Maryann Brinley, Barbara Weller, and Sandra MacGowan — for their positive encouragement. Thanks also go to Nancy Donehower, Bill Hiss, Kristin Crowley, and all those involved in college admissions — staffers and applicants — who shared with me their writing, their experiences, their insights. Thanks also to Bates College, Reed College, Ronald Etergino, Ellen Grosman, David Levi, and Mark Millman for their contributions to Chapter 6. Special thanks to Paul Rossey, Keith Neigel, and the Millburn Board of Education for a leave of absence to do this project.

Finally, I must acknowledge and thank John, J.W., Sarah, Bill, Phyllis, Dorothy, and Valari . . . they know why.

S. M. M.

1

Applying to College

My grandmother was a woman of vision and will. As the eldest child of nine she had to be — and she was *not* going to spend her whole life in Buffalo. Wherever her grit and determination came from, it inspired her, in 1905, to apply to Radcliffe, the women's college at Harvard. She wrote, "I'd like to come." They wrote back, "Come on Monday."

Many things were harder for women in those days, but it seems a few things were easier. In today's world, such a story seems remote, fantastic, and ideal. The college application process is now, like so much else, more complex. Students begin shaping their lives toward college at the beginning of adolescence. Parents have had it in mind from the first day of nursery school.

The process is also noticeably businesslike. It costs a few hundred dollars to travel around and see the colleges you might be interested in, to tour the campuses and have interviews. Add a few hundred dollars more for study books, a review course, tests, and applications. Some seniors will spend a few hundred dollars *more* to get private counseling, specialized advice, coaching for the interviews, help with the applications, or guidance with the essay. All of this is a preamble to the $9,000 to $16,000 a year college itself will cost.

Various companies market assistance. There are SAT review courses in many towns. Bookstores stock review and preparation guides. Publishers issue books on how to beat the tests, how to get into the right school, books full of Madison Avenue ideas like "packaging," "positioning," and "marketing" yourself — as if you were a commercial product jockeying for shelf position, flaunting an appetizing image.

The colleges, too, are eager to present an appealing picture. Many of them create glossy viewbooks, attractive college fair displays, and high school recruiting campaigns to attract top applicants to their campuses.

Many of the people involved in this process, however, lament these changes. Dr. Laura G. Fisher, director of admissions at Harvard University, describes the admissions staff as a group of hard-working people determined "to fashion a community, diverse in expressed interests and talents, that will enable the college to provide the resources, activities, and opportunities the college deems important." But the more common perception is the one described by William C. Hiss, dean of admissions at Bates College: "We are seen, wrongly I think, as a set of intellectual gatekeepers, moral judges, and protectors of the righteous who are already inside. Like Dante's *Divine Comedy*, we offer three possibilities: paradise, purgatory, and hell — that is, admit, wait-list, deny."

The anxiety that such a vision creates for high school students can be intense. To some, colleges seem to be the enemy; they scrutinize and choose without explanation. Acceptance patterns may seem capricious because colleges seek a *diverse* freshman class. There isn't always a clear distinction between The Elect and The Damned. Students who apply for early decision often become the focus of curiosity and concern for other seniors. "How did Jessica get in if Matt didn't?" Juniors carefully watch and analyze the springtime selection of those who precede them. "How could Harvard take Mark when Bowdoin didn't take

Dan?" And some, in moments of panic, conclude that no college is going to admit them. "Remember John last year? He didn't get in anywhere. Guidance was making pitiful phone calls for him all the way into June!"

Making Choices

The purpose of this book is to calm things down a little, because calming down and getting a bit of perspective eases the application process. Understanding the process reduces the anxiety. Knowledge is power. If you know what you're in for, if you know what you are supposed to do and how to do it, you can face the tasks with confidence.

First of all, the goal of this process is not to sell an ideal image of yourself. It is to find the right school for you. The process of choice is almost entirely yours. This is important. *You* are doing nearly all the decision making. Remember, colleges are themselves competing for students. You have much more control in this situation than you imagine. You've been gathering knowledge about colleges for a long time. You've heard of Harvard and

Yale and Stanford . . . and the schools where Mom and Dad or your elder brother or the kid down the block went. You've begun a list of *your choices*. Your guidance counselor may help you add others, but it's your list.

You write for application packets and perhaps take a trip to see some of *your choices*. You narrow down the list, settle on the colleges that really suit you, and then apply to *your choices* — those you're convinced you could be happy at, including a "safety" and one or two "long shots." You are still doing all the choosing.

Then the applications are filed. It is only at this point that the choice is out of your hands. But assuming your selection of colleges is reasonable, you will probably be accepted at more than one school and, once again, the choice will be yours. Each one of the colleges is hopeful that *you* will accept *them*!

Keeping in mind that you're in charge should calm things down somewhat. Your goal is not to gain admission to the most academically grueling institution in America; it is to find a school where you can grow, learn, and succeed, a school where your special talents and interests will be appreciated and cultivated. You will make your choices with information from a wide range of sources:

- guidebooks
- catalogs and literature from the colleges
- reputation
- word of mouth
- alumni and other applicants from your high school
- guidance personnel, teachers, and other professionals
- college representatives at your high school
- campus visits and interviews

Working hard on your part of this job — researching the schools and preparing the applications — will make the part you don't control less threatening and unpredictable.

A close look at what you're not in charge of — the admissions process — may help, too. Colleges are not looking for one type of student. As Dr. Fisher said, they are trying to put together a diverse community. Their goal is remarkably similar to yours: to find a successful match of school and student. It is interesting to compare the way you choose with the way the college chooses. The college relies on a much more focused set of resources:

- grades, class rank, and grade-point average
- course of study
- test scores
- biographical data (summer activities, jobs, special interests)
- recommendations
- an interview
- one or more essays
- where appropriate, supporting material (audition, portfolio)

Each of these elements contributes to the picture of you the college will examine and judge. Of course, the evaluation process differs at every school. Large universities and state schools may not enjoy the luxury of a personalized evaluation of each application. Some tax-supported state universities admit any state resident with passing grades and a high school diploma — Idaho, for example. California state schools declare numerical minimums (for grades, grade-point average, rank in class, and so on) for admission. Computers assist in the process at the University of Texas at Austin; applicants mail in their scores and grades and, if they elect Automatic Decision, a computer issues the appropriate letter. Other schools shun the high-tech approach. The University of Michigan reviews 17,000 applications without computer assistance. Lance Erickson, associate director of admissions at Michigan, says, "Our admissions process is not like that of a small liberal arts college but we do not evaluate our applications with a computer; some applications are, in fact, evaluated three or four times." Colleges may rate applicants' personal and academic qualities, assigning numbers to each of these factors. Bennington, however, does not reduce any part of its 550 applications to a number. All schools, even the large state universities that rely heavily on computers, have a special process for "gray zone" applications which may require additional readers or consideration by a committee. Every college makes its decisions in its own way.

The people who make these decisions also vary. The readers of applications are usually experienced senior admissions personnel and younger staffers, often themselves recent graduates of the school. But faculty members may be part of the process. At Cal Tech, all admissions decisions are made by faculty. Oberlin, Reed, and Sarah Lawrence include student readers on admissions committees. Applicants may also be looked at by specialists: music faculty hear auditions; art staff view portfolios. A dean of admissions oversees everything.

The committee is not a nameless, faceless group of people, uniform in taste and attitude. It is made up of individuals. Assigned a seemingly endless pile of folders in the dark days of early spring, such an audience — overworked and tired — may find that a creative, innovative, interesting, or unique element in an application makes the difference. High scores and great grades do stand out. But students mistake their audience when they visualize a stuffy bunch of academics in search of an academic superstar. Donald Heider, associate director of admissions at Franklin and Marshall College, says, "We're not looking for one kind of student. A liberal arts college would be ill-advised to do that." There is no perfect applicant. Many things are sought within a class and many different elements make up the admissions committee's final judgment. The folder is a web of information, a jigsaw puzzle that is interconnected and interactive. Each element plays its own part, each makes its own argument.

Your High School Record

The numbers come first. Colleges request grades beginning with ninth grade. Three and a half years of performance gives them a knowledge of your academic achievement and also a look at the pattern of your growth and progress. Straight A's are nice — but very rare in a challenging course of study. An improvement in grades is positive, too — the opposite will certainly raise eyebrows in the admissions office. But above all other factors in the grade pattern, most colleges scrutinize the course load. A grade of B in Advanced Placement English is more important than an A in Chorus. An A in chemistry carries more weight than an A in civics. Dr. Robert W. Spencer, dean of admissions and records at Brigham Young University, describes how BYU considers course choices: "We add a factor to a student's grades for a strong educational program and for more challenging courses; we will consider up to 70 percent of the applicant's program in this way." Grades, class rank, and grade-point average are viewed in light of your course choices.

Grades, class rank, and grade-point average are also viewed in terms of your high school and its student body. Colleges assign regional responsibility to members of the admissions staff who familiarize themselves with a few states or with one part of the country. They get to know the high schools and their course offerings. Some secondary schools have a reputation for excellence; others have less rigorous programs. Each school's general quality is considered in evaluating class rank and course of study.

Scores

A testing service also contributes numbers to your application. Schools usually require either the Scholastic Aptitude Test (SAT) and Achievement Tests or the American College Testing Program Assessment (ACT). These standardized tests help admissions personnel evaluate applicants' abilities relative to successful performance in college. The scores are seen as a yardstick with which students of widely differing backgrounds can be compared.

You probably took the PSAT/NMSQT or practiced with books like *10 SATs*. Some high schools offer SAT review courses as part of the curriculum and some students take a private review course. Familiarizing yourself with the various types of test questions can

put you at ease and may make you a more efficient test taker.

The admissions committee will look at your scores and compare them to your grades. High grades can overcome low scores but admissions personnel will carefully scrutinize the course load and the high school's reputation. High scores can sometimes compensate for low grades, but that particular combination tends to make admissions personnel nervous: Does the student lack motivation? Is she just a bright goof-off?

Grades, course load, grade-point average, class rank, and scores are the numerical information colleges use to evaluate an application. They look to your past as a clue to your future. Studies show that neither grades nor test scores alone indicate whether an applicant will succeed in college. However, the combination of high school record *and* scores has been found to be a fairly valid indicator of college success. College work also relies on the same study habits, self-discipline, skills, and personal qualities — enthusiasm, organization, independence of thought, responsibility, perseverance — that you need in high school. A lot of these qualities also contribute to success in a career.

Select colleges with all your high school numbers in mind. Don't let yourself become overwhelmed by standardized test scores. Remember that the numbers colleges list are usually the *median* scores, not the cut-off scores. If a school lists its median SAT verbal score as 600, then 50 percent of the class scored higher than 600, and *50 percent scored lower.* In 1985, Princeton listed its average SAT mathematics score for those enrolled as 692. Therefore, many students who were admitted did not score 692. In fact, Princeton admitted four students whose math scores fell between 400 and 449! Now perhaps some of those students had 800 on the verbal section of the SAT. But somewhere in Princeton's class of 1989 there is a student who got a 430 in the mathematical section!

Numbers are only part of your application. They will, however, help you determine which schools are, for you, long shots and which are likely to be satisfied with your performance. They will help the admissions committee determine if you are a sure accept, a clear deny, or a maybe.

Other sections of the application are less numerical. *Personal Qualities and College Admissions* (College Entrance Examination Board, 1982), Warren Willingham and Hunter Breland's study of applicants to nine different colleges, showed that personal qualities are also a valid indicator of college success; colleges look to the recommendations, essays, and interview to give them a sense of the person. Some colleges, like Bennington, consider these elements the primary criteria in an evaluation.

Recommendations

Evaluations will be written by your high school counselor and by a few of your teachers. Make them more effective by scheduling an early appointment with your counselor to discuss your college selection. If your high school is large and your relationship with your counselor a bit remote (the national ratio of students to counselors last year ranged between 140 to 1 and 478 to 1), you might prepare a simple life history or a résumé for your counselor. It's good preparation for filling out the applications and, by listing some of your circumstances and activities, you help your counselor write a specific and informed recommendation.

Approach your teachers early. Ask for recommendations from teachers who like you, for whom you have done well, whose courses relate to your intended area of specialization, and who are themselves articulate, careful, and responsible. You want a positive letter and one that will be consistent with the rest of your application. But don't forget that such a letter isn't likely to be written by even your favorite teacher if he or she is overworked, hassled, and pressed for time. Ask your teachers directly, "Do you have the time to write a strong recommendation letter for me for Bucknell?" Name the school, because that may influence their response. There are students a teacher would happily recommend to a state school who should not expect the same enthusiasm toward an application to Stanford. And don't be downcast if the teacher says he or she is too busy or can't do it. Approach someone else. You don't want your letter gathering dust on the desk of a teacher who *meant* to do it but had too many periods of cafeteria duty to find the time.

You might want to give the teachers your brief résumé. They will rely mostly on what you've done in their classes, but it helps if they know you were entering piano competitions or working nights at McDonald's while you were turning out first-rate reports on Jacksonian democracy. Give the recommending teacher a list of the courses you took with him or her, the grades you received, and any special projects or major papers you did. Students come and go and most teachers appreciate a little memory-jogging. Be sure to provide stamped, addressed envelopes, and fill out all the parts of the form indicated as the student's responsibility. Waive your right of access; it shows confidence in your recommender and adds credibility to the letter.

The Interview

Now for the tricky stuff. The numbers are behind you. What you've done in high school is settled. Don't expend energy or worry over things you can't change: the school you attended, the C+ you earned in English II. There are grades to be earned for the senior year and this is certainly no time to coast. But most of the numbers your high school will send to the colleges are fixed. Your recommendations are in the works. The last part of your evaluation will be drawn from an interview and from the essay.

The interview, whether on campus or with a local alumni interviewer, is one chance to present yourself personally to the college. But the interview is usually rather brief and can be intimidating. At one interview, Bernard M. Ravina, now a freshman at Columbia, was asked, "What do you see when you get up in the morning and look in the mirror?" Ravina reflects: "He was digging for something . . . I was thrown off by the question. He really got on my nerves." Ravina found the best preparation was to go into interviews with a specific sense of what he wanted to emphasize about himself and a set of questions about the school that were not answered in the catalog.

Drafting a résumé may make you comfortable with questions about your academic career and activities. Many of the questions are similar to those asked on the application, so you might want to look over or complete your applications before beginning the interviews. It helps to have one interview at a college that is courting you; you need to feel needed at about this time. Schedule the most important interview late in the sequence; you'll be more experienced and confident.

Do your "homework" and use the interviewer's knowledge of the college to help you get to know the school better. Robert Steadman, a senior recently accepted at Columbia, Dartmouth, Oberlin, and Yale, advises, "Be ready for anything, but work at making the interview valuable for you. I tried to go into the interviews with an open mind and roll with the punches. But I had questions ready, too. When the alumni interviewer from

Columbia asked, 'Why Columbia?' I asked 'Why do *you* think Columbia is the place to apply? What made *you* go there?' " The better your questions, the better the impression you will make and the more useful the interview will be to you. Questions already answered in the catalog waste the interviewer's and your time. Questions about the social life or how many students stay on campus during the weekend are better asked during the campus tour. Make your questions a little aggressive. It's much better to ask "Would you send your child to this school?" than "Do you have a major in computer science?"

The interview is a two-way street, not just an opportunity to impress the admissions personnel. Don Heider, at Franklin and Marshall, says, "It's the seller's one chance to show the consumer where he ought to spend his $50,000." Use the interview to assess further the fit between you and the school, to learn if you want to choose it.

The interview is not always required and not every school you interview with will take it seriously. Sometimes you have only half an hour to make an impression and gather information, and the first ten minutes is often spent getting oriented and trying to relax ("Did you find a parking place? How long a drive was it?"). Some interviewers find students too shy or guarded to be accurately assessed in a short, high-pressure meeting. Like the recommendations, the value of the interview may vary. Interviews are becoming less practical with the size and geographic range of most applicant pools. Interviews have been dropped at Stanford and are giving way to mass information sessions at many other schools, such as Brown and Vassar.

The Essay

The essay, however, is still taken as a significant and reliable source of information about the applicant. Gayle Moskowitz, a high school counselor in New Jersey, says, "The better the college, the more heavily they weigh the essay." A number of colleges — Bennington, for example — rank the essay as a primary source of information. For liberal arts majors applying to

Northwestern University, it is second only to performance in the high school course program. Some colleges make it optional, or look at it only in "gray zone" cases. Even at the University of Michigan, which receives approximately 17,000 applications, the essay is always read.

Admissions committees use the essay to get to know the student in a more reliable, specific, and personal way than the numbers and recommendations provide. Robert Grinnell, assistant dean of admissions at Gordon College, says, "For us, the essay is a critical component in the application. We're looking for a special commitment and the essay gives us something the numbers don't reveal."

Nancy Siegel, a high school guidance counselor, agrees: "Colleges want a third dimension. Without the essay, the application profile is flat." Even Brigham Young University, with a fairly homogeneous applicant pool, finds diversity in the essays. The university asks applicants why they have chosen Brigham Young; since most applicants are members of the Church of Jesus Christ of Latter-day Saints, one might expect a fairly uniform response, but as Robert Spencer notes, "Although all our applicants say they want to come to BYU for the education and for the right spiritual atmosphere, this is said in many different ways. The essay can tell us about the thought process, the maturity of thinking, purposes, and goals." The application is a jigsaw puzzle; each part contributes a piece to the overall picture.

What does the essay contribute? Choice is very important here. The process of choosing an answer, and often a question, is central to all college essays. Choice shows something about what and how you think. William Hiss, at Bates College, says, "The essay may help us see and judge the depth of the student's understanding of intellectual or social issues but it also shows the quality and freshness of the applicant's mind." It can show priorities, values, the ability to synthesize and connect, the ability to get something out of an experience.

The essay adds a personal, human element to the application. It can breathe life into your activities, interests, experiences, or family situation, making these elements real and vivid. Nancy Donehower, assistant dean of admissions at Reed College, says, "For me the essay is the most important part of the application. For a small college with a personal approach rather than an 'acceptability quotient,' it's the place where the kid can strut his stuff. It tells you a lot about character. It can reveal the person who likes to learn because he likes learning or the person who finds the process greater than the product. It can show how analytical the applicant is. If he says his summer in France taught him to observe cultural differences, and then says, 'For example, in France the cars are a lot smaller,' this gives us a good idea of how little he's thought about and analyzed his life experiences."

The essay can be an explanation of grades or exceptional circumstances in your background. If your grades and scores are not reflective of your ability, if your numbers don't tell all, the essay is your chance to make that clear. (Remember, if there are very special circumstances in your life — an illness, a family situation, a handicap — be sure to tell the college about this. Submit an essay on this subject whether it's asked for or not.)

The essay also shows what a student will do with an opportunity:

Did she pass it up and use a predictable, prepackaged sentiment?

"I chose Carleton College because Carleton is committed to learning and I want to learn."

Did he take it seriously?

Dartmouth asks you to create an ideal application question and answer it; they do not learn much from responses like "Are you having a nice day?" or "Should this applicant be accepted? YES!!!"

Did she take risks?

"These are the voyages of the Starship Nussbaum."

Did he get Mom to do it for him?

Admissions people usually can tell.

The essay is particularly useful in determining the fit between the applicant and the college. Success at any school depends on knowing what you're in for; nothing is more bitter than disappointed expectations. Peter Richardson, director of admissions at Bennington, says, "One of the critical issues for Bennington is the match between the student and the philosophy of the college, a match that is not necessarily revealed through the numbers. We look to the essay, the interview, and the recommendations for this information." Most colleges seek something like this "match." If a college has a particular character — it's progressive or relies on a very special kind of teaching method or curriculum — the essay can reflect your suitability for its special setting: St. John's, West Point, or Hampshire, for example.

Next, the essay shows your writing abilities — organization, analysis, interpretation — and your mastery of the conventions of standard written English. Writing — essays and tests — is important in college. Keith Boone, assistant director of admissions at Oberlin, began requiring a school essay in support of Oberlin applications; Occidental and Vassar do the same. Other schools encourage applicants to submit writing samples. Since your ability to interpret, analyze, and express yourself clearly, correctly, and vividly will be crucial in most of your college courses, your college essay will be looked at in these terms. Sarah Lawrence rates student writing ability on the basis of the essay, assigning each applicant a 0, 1, or 2. How you write as well as what you write is important to admissions.

The essay is particularly important for "gray zone" applications. These folders are often discussed by committees of readers. An exceptional element gives a staffer a basis upon which to defend an applicant's admission. Can an essay get a student in? According to James Montoya, director of admissions at Vassar, "Yes, it can. Not a student with a very poor record but it can sway a reader and get an application to the committee for further consideration." At Bates, "The essay can be a powerful 'tipper' in close cases, especially with very strong or very poor essays."

The essay is the part of the application that most effectively personalizes your self-presentation. The recommendations are sometimes questioned, the interview is becoming less common and more of a momentary "snapshot." The essay is the only aspect of the application process that is still open to development and is safely in *your* hands. It is an opportunity to show the admissions committee a little about yourself, your insights, your enthusiasm, your writing ability. The essay is also an opportunity to convey, under less pressure and with more preparation than the interview, something of your personal style; it counteracts the numbers and the anonymity of the application process.

The essay fits into the overall pattern of your application. The colleges take it seriously; you should, too. It is part of your need to compete and the college's need to select. If an essay is required or even allowed, use it to present yourself effectively. It is a *separate* part of the application and should convey information not found elsewhere. If you ignore this advice, you defeat the college's purpose in requesting an essay.

Seize this opportunity to stand out from the better numbers, the similar recommendations, the other kids. Don't default on it; don't give it away. It's a wonderful opportunity to speak out for yourself in that dark, dusty room of folders. It's not so terrible and it's not so hard. You've actually done plenty of papers like it already!

A Time Line for Applying to College

Junior Year

1. Visit college fairs, talk to friends and alumni; look at various college guides and ask counselors and teachers for suggestions.
2. Write for catalogs and see what the colleges say they want.

3. Take the PSAT/NMSQT; take Achievement Tests at the end of appropriate courses of study.
4. Consider visiting colleges in the spring or over the summer.
5. Mention your plans to the teachers you may want to have write your recommendations.
6. Take the SATs in the spring.
7. Consider keeping a journal or collecting interesting "important moment" articles from your reading as samples for your essay.

Senior Year

SEPTEMBER

1. Attend college conferences at your high school.
2. Set up campus visits and interviews.
3. Take more Achievement Tests; you may want to retake the SATs.
4. Line up your recommending teachers.
5. Request application packets from the colleges that interest you.

OCTOBER

1. Confirm your choices with your counselor.
2. Give recommending teachers letters, envelopes, a résumé.
3. Pool application essay questions by type (see Chapter 4); begin thinking about the questions.

NOVEMBER

1. Fill out applications.
2. Begin essays, using the process described in Chapter 5.

DECEMBER

1. Finish essays and copy or type them onto the applications. PROOFREAD YOUR ESSAYS AT LEAST TWICE!!
2. Mail applications early and feel self-righteous as your friends scurry and panic.

2

What You Know About Essay Writing

A New but Familiar Assignment

When the application packets begin to arrive, the anxiety builds. It was fun looking at the photographs, reading the course offerings, and fantasizing about next fall. But the burden of choice is shifting from the schools you choose to the schools that will choose *you*.

As described in Chapter 1, much of the data for this decision is settled. Grades have been recorded, scores reported, recommendation letters provided. But the essay is yet to be written. The application you're filling out may ask for a list of the items you'd include in a time capsule; or perhaps you've been asked to describe lunch with a famous person. Even a straightforward essay about yourself may seem intimidating; it may seem as if you've never done anything like this before. Your teachers assigned papers and reports, with topics such as the theme of love in a particular novel or the causes of a given war. This may appear to be a very different business.

But think about it for a moment and you'll realize that you have, in fact, done this assignment before — *many* times. All those papers for English class — and for history, and even for science — were essentially like the college essay. And even if the college essay seems harder, it isn't. It's different — and in many ways it's easier.

The Challenge of the College Essay

As you have seen in the first chapter, the essay is a special opportunity to introduce yourself. You have an attentive audience that believes this part of your application will give useful additional information, a different and reliable lens on you. And although the admissions committee will not choose or reject you on the basis of this single element, the essay can be a strong voice in your favor, a way to stand out from the rest, a determining factor for a "gray zone" application. According to Peter Richardson at Bennington, "We'll take a risk for the right reason." Sometimes it is the essay that gives them that reason. So while admissions people want to hear from your high school counselors and teachers, they also want to hear from *you.*

The college essay should be, in one way or another, an essay of self-analysis. Self-analysis is not easy and it can be especially hard to do at this point in your life, when many of your goals and plans are unsettled. You may already have confronted this problem at the interviews. Admissions people ask, "Tell us about yourself" or "What are your hopes and aspirations?" These are questions that require self-analysis, and they're pretty hard. The college has questions about you partly because you still have questions about yourself. But the essay is a chance to demonstrate which questions you've asked yourself and what answers you've found.

The college, then, is asking you to do something genuinely difficult — tell about yourself — and here the pressure is really on. The audience is critical and crucial; readers unknown to you intend to take your performance seriously.

The essay is also going to be examined as a clue to your writing ability. Columbia University lets you know what they're looking for right on the application: "Please remember that we are concerned not only with the substance of your prose but with your writing as well." Kristin Crowley, who read essays at Yale for three years, is equally direct: "Of course the essay is seen as an index to student writing. After all, a very large part of your performance and evaluation in college will be based on essays and written tests. Skill in essay writing is essential to success in a competitive liberal arts college. The essay portion of the application is one way to find out if prospective students have one of the basic skills they'll need when they're here." Carol Lunkenheimer, director of admissions at Northwestern, sees the essay as a useful defense of a student's acceptability. "It is greatly in an applicant's favor if the reader can say, 'This kid can write.'"

So the challenge is to have your own say with power and precision. *You* in one page! Clearly there is pressure here and it is natural for anything that is challenging to be threatening as well at times. But with yourself as the subject, you actually have all it takes to succeed!

The Structure

A college essay is nothing new; it is the type of writing with which you are most familiar. Let's look at your writing skills and the kind of writing you have learned in the last 12 years.

First of all, it was organized — your paper on *The Great Gatsby* had a format, as did your papers for history and science. They had a beginning, a middle, and an end. You did not just ramble. You focused on a single point and stuck to it, describing and developing your insights and observations. At the end, you returned to your main idea, which you summarized and refocused.

A paragraph on the economic causes of the Civil War might have looked like this:

Beginning: Some of the causes of the Civil War were economic
Middle: A sentence or two on Northern prosperity
  A sentence or two on Southern agricultural economy
  Three or four sentences on the conflicts these different economies created in trade, standard of living, relations with England
End: A concluding sentence

A paper on *The Great Gatsby* might have been like this:

Beginning: *The Great Gatsby* explores different kinds of love
Middle: A paragraph about friendship
    Daisy and Jordan
    Gatsby and Nick
  A paragraph about false love
    Nick and Jordan
    Myrtle and Tom
  A paragraph about true love
    Gatsby and Daisy
End: Summary/conclusion

A science paper might have looked like this:

Main idea: Desert animals show a significant adaptation to their environment
Body:
  A paragraph about adjustment to heat/cold:
    burrowing animals
    cold-blooded animals
  A paragraph about adjustment to weather:
    natural protections from sandstorms
    natural protections from dehydration

A paragraph about adjustment to limited food:
storing nourishment
extracting water
Conclusion: A summary or conclusion drawn from the above

The structure of formal writing has been described in this way:

Tell 'em what you're gonna tell 'em
Tell 'em
Tell 'em what you told 'em

This is a good way to think of your writing. The three parts are a natural way to present any topic. After all, you are leading the reader along an unfamiliar path. You have to give that reader an idea of the basic subject so he can focus his attention. The middle will be meaningful if he's got a focus to follow; he can keep an eye out for love or economic factors. Likewise, with a reiteration or closing comment at the end, you strengthen the coherence of your argument.

You've used this three-part pattern in a variety of situations.

The paragraph
Topic sentence
Development
End sentence

The essay
Introduction
Body
Conclusion

No matter what your writing background, you have worked with this common structural pattern. It has been part of your school curriculum for a number of years and it is something you have practiced. It is a skill that seems to come naturally to most writers when they want to explain something or describe an idea unfamiliar to their readers. Even work on the school newspaper or personal writing may have given you practice in this three-part format:

> Dear Joe,
> My summer vacation was a blast. Here is what we did .... It was really the best.
> Love,
> Jennifer

You have been taught this structure, and it is just what you need for the college essay. (Sample 1 in Chapter 6 is a good example.) It is also the underlying structure of a lot of college writing, business writing, journal articles, proposals, reports, and speeches. If you're a bit shaky about how it works, pay careful attention to Chapter 3 because you'll need this skill now *and later*.

The Style

You're experienced with the structure you'll need for the essay, and there's more good news: You have also had 12 years of experience with the style. You know the difference between academic and personal writing, between term papers and diaries, between essays and love letters.

Everyone has a natural storehouse of different styles of speech and of writing. You talk to the person taking your order at the local pizza parlor with a very different vocabulary and style than you would use if a corporate receptionist asked, "May I help you?" So you automatically write for each assignment in a different way. Without being conscious of it, you use a style and vocabulary for a paper on *Hamlet* that is nothing like what you'd use in writing a note to Mom. You know you have to check your spelling and you automatically strive for the level of vocabulary and correctness suitable for a finished piece of work.

> Hamlet is like really wacko. The guy just can't get over his old man's kicking off so he fakes being out of it most of the time.

Pretty funny. The humor is a result of mismatching style and situation. Most writers move back and forth between various levels of language and styles of writing as easily as they adapt their speech to their listeners. You know the right level of language for a given situation and you know the college essay is a serious piece of writing. It is also not quite as formal as most school writing; you'll want all the clarity and correctness you can produce but, considering the subject (you), you'll also want a slightly more direct and personal tone than you might otherwise use. Your spelling and sentence structure should be correct but your word choice and style should not be heavily academic, full of thesaurus words, or unnatural for you.

You also have a good idea of what your strengths and weaknesses are as a writer. (If you want more information, look at your writing folder from last semester, or ask your English teacher.) You have plenty of time to proofread, look up potential problem words, and edit your essay. The flow of good ideas is interrupted by dum errers; save time to proofread thoroughly and correct your own dumb errors.

You certainly have adequate motivation built into this situation. It's only a matter of diligence to bring your performance to perfection and, again, you've had 12 years of practice.

The Subject

The greatest strength you bring to this essay has been 17 years or so in the making: YOU. The form and style are very familiar, and

best of all, you are the world-class expert on the subject.

You really know a lot about you. If you can write about wars, novels, experiments, and sonnets, writing about yourself should be simple. You don't have to do any research. You don't have to study the major city-states of the Renaissance or read *Macbeth.* You already know all you need to know. And there is a wealth of information, thousands of incidents, events, and facts, from which to draw. Instead of being at a loss for material, you may find the quantity a little overwhelming. However, you don't have to despair of finding a topic; it has been the subject of your close scrutiny every morning since you were tall enough to see into the bathroom mirror.

Another wonderful aspect of this topic is that no one else has it; it is unique. No essay will directly compete with yours. You've picked colleges that are appropriate for you, probably a group of similar schools that include a "long shot" and a "sure thing." They are tailored to you and you are, therefore, tailored to them. Your desires, plans, and abilities probably fall within a profile of each college's student body, so your essay has every reason to stand up to the other submissions.

Remember, the colleges are not looking for a single answer. Admissions personnel do not look for a specific student. There is no set combination of items that every applicant must have to gain acceptance at a certain college. You, your essay, and your application profile do not have to match a single narrow standard. They need only fit into one of the constituencies, into the larger pattern of students at your chosen school.

The best part of the college essay is that it can't be *wrong*. One of my students wrote an entire paper on "The Love Song of J. Alfred Prufrock" as if it were a poem set in an aquarium. It turned out she had read the line about the yellow fog and thought it was "the yellow frog" that pressed its nose against the window pane! But had she said she loved aquariums, who could possibly question that? Everyone laughed at the boy who thought "On First Looking into Chapman's Homer" was about baseball, but an essay on his lunch with Don Mattingly would be a different story. Follow the advice of Elizabeth DeLaHunt at Sarah Lawrence College: "Take a deep breath, relax, and believe in yourself." There is no fixed critical opinion about you, no standard theory of interpretation. You can't come off looking bad because you didn't know that Jake's war wound was impotence, that Hamlet's problem was melancholia, that "Stopping by Woods on a Snowy Evening" is about suicide. You don't have to do research. You have had lots of experience with this "text" and you are really the major authority in the field.

The topic may seem hard, but it's really the essay's greatest attraction. It's about you — a topic you know, need to know, want to talk about, have as your exclusive territory, and can't be wrong about. You are the real expert and can easily speak with both authority and conviction.

The Process

Finally, the process of all school papers is the process you will use, and not only as far as the steps to follow. Of course, you will want to brainstorm a little, organize a lot, write, rewrite, and edit; a guide to the composition process is given in Chapter 3. But, the thought process is the same as well: focus and prove.

Let's look back at that paper on *The Great Gatsby*. You chose or were assigned a topic: love. You narrowed it down to a manageable size: three major points. Then you explored the novel and drew out the incidents that proved Fitzgerald portrayed different kinds of love. You gathered as many examples as made your point vivid and then described them to the extent that they supported your theme.

The application of this process to the college essay is simple. In this case, you look into your life, select an element, event, experience, or insight, and assign a meaning to it: that fateful summer, that wonderful biology class, that meaningful job at the ice cream parlor, that exciting lunch I might have had with Charles Darwin. Then you prove the validity of that meaning, backing up and substantiating the view you have taken.

Thus the standard school essay is good preparation for writing a college essay. Academic topics aren't so far from college essay topics. Both are often based on the isolation of a single aspect of some dense and complex phenomenon. A war, a novel, a food chain may be good for a day's lesson. But these are too much for an essay topic, and *so are you.* No teacher has asked you to write on a topic like, "Tell me everything you know about Napoleon"; the college doesn't want to hear *all* about you either. Avoid a sort of shotgun approach; telling everything about yourself is not the idea. Select *one* thing about yourself and illuminate that. The light from one interesting point will reflect a lot about your entire personality. Less is more here. A small and interesting facet will shine most brightly.

The idea is not so much to be different or noble or scholarly. It is better to be vivid and clear. What you want to show is your intensity, enthusiasm, insight, and understanding. This is, after all, what the college wants to see. It's what they hope to measure in the essay and what you'll need to succeed when you're accepted.

Don't panic. You have all the skills you need and the assignment is your best and favorite topic. Your school essays have been your training ground for the right structure, style, and process. The next chapter reviews the process of writing an essay. Chapters 4 and 5 take a look at the college essay questions and present different strategies for making the most of this special essay, an opportunity to introduce yourself to a college.

3

How To Write an Essay

The purpose of this chapter is to review the process of writing any essay. You may be experienced enough with this form to skim this chapter quickly and go right on to Chapters 4 and 5, which apply the general form to the application essay. Check the summary page at the end of this chapter. If the concepts there seem unfamiliar, or if writing has not been your strength in high school, you will want to read and study this chapter carefully before writing the essays for your applications and again when you begin writing essays in college.

What Exactly Is an Essay?

Essays are as diverse as writers themselves and do not conform to as specific a pattern as sonnets or tragedies or lab reports. However, most essays are some sort of a defense of a writer's opinion or point of view. The opinions vary greatly: Shakespeare's plays all deal with the restoration of order; Springfield ought to build a youth activity center; the United States should no longer invest its tax monies in manned space exploration; gerbils need a stable social environment to flourish; U2 is the most innovative rock group around today.

Personal and particular or academic and distant, the essay tries to convince the reader that an opinion, theory, or interpretation is correct. Thus an essay can be a newspaper editorial advocating reduced taxes, a term paper on *The Great Gatsby* as a tragedy, a proposal from an architectural firm for a shopping mall, or a defense of an innocent client in a court of law. The college essay, too, presents a thesis — a view of the applicant — to the college admissions board, and persuades them of its validity. Actually, a great deal of writing involves proving a thesis.

Writing any essay is a process. There are stages and steps to follow. The writer who makes multiple drafts and the one who rarely revises both go through a similar process, either on paper or in their heads. But like Abraham Lincoln, who scribbled a few notes on an envelope on his way to Gettysburg, most writers prefer to complete some of the preliminary steps on paper. The process is:

1. Some preparation and prewriting
2. A number of drafts (from one to several)
3. Some revising and editing

A 45-minute final examination essay in modern European history might involve:

1. Two minutes of preparation
2. Forty minutes on the single draft you will write
3. Three minutes of quick proofreading and revising

The final essay or term paper for the same course would involve:

1. A few days of planning and preparation, with research in the library
2. Two drafts or more

3. Editing and revising; optional review by another reader — a friend, relative, or peer tutor at your school's writing center

The examination essay takes less than an hour; the term paper, one to two weeks. However, the three-part process is used in both writing situations.

Writing as a Process
Prewriting
Drafting
Editing

Prewriting

The goal of prewriting is to develop your focus; it has four aspects:

1. Brainstorming
2. Grouping and revising
3. Focusing
4. Organizing

Brainstorming

It's time to clean your room. Throw everything that's not nailed down into a heap in the center: books, clothes, albums, letters, used coffee cups, Twinkie wrappers. Now you have a sense of how much you have to do and exactly with what you have to work. Piles can be sorted from the central mess — one for the laundry, one to be saved, one to go in the trash, and so on.

Many writers like to begin with a similar fast and disorganized collection of potential ideas. They throw every possible idea into one place and then look at it. Patterns, groups, and an overall sense of what they have to work with begin to emerge. This is brainstorming.

Take a piece of paper (or work on a computer if you can).

Write the limits of your assignment on the top of the page: 750 words on my summer vacation, a paragraph on the importance of the Wagner Act, a 3- to 5-page paper on *Macbeth,* a 10-page paper on Jacksonian democracy and modern populism. Now write down everything you can think of that relates to the topic. List single words that pop into your mind. Ask yourself questions about the topic, make statements, wonder, speculate, recall, and connect. Set a timer or otherwise establish a time limit so that you will keep on writing for several minutes. Do not stop to daydream or reread. Just write, write, write.

Here are two different samples of students' three-minute brainstorms on the singer Bruce Springsteen:

SAMPLE 1.

> Bruce: sings about what he believes in — *Born in the USA* — how he feels — good concerts (4 hours) — been around a while — hasn't really appealed to me — not so hung up on fame — takes it as it comes — recently married to Julianne Phillips — just finished worldwide tour with new album — will probably soon have another album out — only a few songs impress me.

(This student jotted down a stream-of-consciousness response of facts and personal feelings about the topic.)

SAMPLE 2.

> Grew up in Freehold, New Jersey
>
> Became famous in Asbury Park, New Jersey clubs . . . The Stone Pony
>
> In 1975 made the covers of *Time* and *Newsweek* with hit album *Born to Run*
>
> *Born in the USA*

Hit songs on *BTR:* "Born to Run"
"Thunder Road"

"Jungleland"

Hit songs in *Born in the USA:* almost all of them

Had a 16-month tour — 1984-85 — for album

Concerts

Recently married

Rumson

USA for Africa

"We Are the World" song and video

"Jersey Girl"

Steve Van Zandt and *Sun City*

Sings about his life and things he's familiar with

(This student is more knowledgeable about the topic; she began with a chronological approach and produced a list of facts rather than a personal response.)

This stream-of-consciousness collecting process can begin without paper and pencil. Some writers mull over an idea for days or weeks or even years. But a significant percentage of writers use a journal, diary, or notebook: They write as a way to begin thinking about writing. Nathaniel Hawthorne, for one, kept such a journal.

> The life of a woman, who, by the old colony law, was condemned always to wear the letter A, sewed on her garment, in token of her having committed adultery.

The beginning of *The Scarlet Letter,* and quite a few other Hawthorne stories, can be traced to the brainstorming he did in this journal. So, for many writing assignments, the way to begin (especially if beginning is difficult and you aren't sure where to begin) is to brainstorm thoughts and responses to the assignment and see exactly with what you have to work. This can be a quick preparation for writing (as for a final examination) or, if you have the luxury of time, you can add to your brainstorm and collect ideas for quite a while before you go on to the next step.

Grouping and Revising

After you have discovered that you do know something about your subject, that you do have a few ideas and questions, go over the brainstorming sheet and look for connections or connectable ideas. You are moving toward a focus. In the second Bruce Springsteen brainstorm, for example, there are some song titles, facts about the singer's life, and various references to New Jersey.

Grew up in Freehold, New Jersey
Became famous in Asbury, New Jersey clubs . . . The Stone Pony
In 1975 made the covers of *Time* and *Newsweek* with hit album *Born to Run*
Born in the USA
Hit songs on *BTR:* "Born to Run"
"Thunder Road"
SONGS — "Jungleland"
Hit songs in *Born in the USA:* almost all of them
Had a 16-month tour — 1984-1985 — for album
Concerts
Recently married — BIOGRAPHY
Rumson
USA for Africa
"We Are the World" song and video — NEW JERSEY
"Jersey Girl"
Steve Van Zandt and *Sun City*
Sings about his life and things he's familiar with

Any one of these could lead to a topic and then to a thesis for an essay.

Go over the brainstorm sheet several times, adding any new ideas that come to you. Try to identify more themes or patterns among the items you've listed. Most important, ask yourself questions:

- Why are these songs so popular?
- Are they all the same or are they all different?
- Does Springsteen's life have anything to do with his success?
- Why doesn't he live in a big city?
- Why do so many of his songs refer to New Jersey?
- Is he just a local boy made good, or is he an international star who happens to be from New Jersey?

What you are doing now is *analyzing* your topic, breaking it down into pieces. Bruce Springsteen is too much for an essay; better to concentrate on one element of his popularity, his music, or his life. An English essay, for example, might focus on one element of a poem: form, language, setting, tone, theme. A history essay on a president might focus on one campaign strategy, one conflict with Congress, one area of impact. A college essay might focus on one job, one experience, one aspect of your personality. Ask questions:

- Why is this important?
- What is the purpose or function of this one element?
- Why did this occur?
- What was the impact of this one event, decision, choice?

All kinds of questions can lead to topics and move you toward a focus and a plan.

Focusing

You need to get down to work now. Your essay must prove a single point or thesis. If this is a 45-minute midterm, latch onto the first topic that jumps off the page and get to the writing as quickly as possible. If this is an out-of-class essay, you need to develop your own thesis. You will shift and adjust this thesis as you work on other parts of your essay, but one angle or aspect of a large and complex topic is your beginning. Look at the groups and clusters of ideas you have come up with and try making statements about some of them.

- Bruce Springsteen's popularity comes from the diversity of his music.
- Bruce Springsteen is essentially a New Jersey phenomenon.
- Bruce Springsteen sings about New Jersey but his music has a national appeal.

These are preliminary thesis statements and any one of them is a good start: each focuses on an aspect of Bruce Springsteen and asserts an opinion or view about him and his music.

One interesting sentence can be the basis of a persuasive argument. From the groups of ideas on the brainstorm sheet and the questions you've asked yourself, make your own list of possible thesis statements. If time allows, consult with your teacher or professor about these possible topics. If a full-length research paper is the assignment, a trip to the library's card catalog, reader's guides, and indexes in your field might supplement the brainstorming process and help you narrow down and select a topic. Choose the topic that most interests you, the topic about which you have the most to say, the most specific topic you can devise; then get on to the business of making a simple plan.

Organizing

You have chosen a focus; you have a tentative thesis statement. Now you need a plan of attack. You probably are not ready to create a final outline, but it is wise to impose a little order at this point. You need to determine how you will prove your thesis.

Revise your brainstorm sheet and eliminate ideas unrelated to your topic. It may be painful to cross items out, but you can't include everything. A paper that includes *everything* is not an essay; it's still just a brainstorm. Some students write everything they know and hope the teacher will hunt through it and find what he or she wants! Better to prove a small point than require the *reader* to find the meaning in a jumble of information. Take out the red pen and start cutting.

If time and the assignment dictate, you should research your topic. Reread the primary source material, consult critical sources, talk again with your teacher. Begin to line up possible evidence to support your proposed thesis statement.

Once you are satisfied that you have adequate information, rearrange your brainstorm sheet into a tentative list of points or supporting ideas for your topic. Here are three samples of early organizational efforts that include a preliminary thesis and a general plan of proof to be covered in the essay:

Shakespeare's plays deal with the restoration of order

1. *Romeo and Juliet:* the conflict between the Capulets and the Montagues must give way to peace and order
2. *The Taming of the Shrew:* Kate's aggressive attempts to dominate men must yield to a more orderly and peaceful relationship between men and women
3. *Hamlet:* Hamlet's burden is the ghost's command that he restore order by revenging his father's murder

Gerbils need a stable social environment to flourish

1. The control group
    a. eating habits
    b. growth
    c. behavior
    d. mating habits
2. The experimental group
    a. eating habits
    b. growth
    c. behavior
    d. mating habits

Bruce Springsteen belongs to New Jersey

1. Songs about New Jersey
2. Biographical proof
3. Involvement with the workers' cause in Freehold
4. State song proposal

As you create a simple outline, choose an appropriate order for your points. One common organizational plan is by time: Discuss a process step by step, the events in a novel in the order in which they happened, the plays of Shakespeare in the order in which they were written.

Another possible organizational plan is by location. Chaucer often described a Canterbury pilgrim's head and face first, the garments next, the horse last. So might a paper present building sites one after another, describe a view from left to right, or compare two cages of gerbils, one at a time.

The most useful order of points in an essay is from least to most important. Remember that the goal of an essay is to persuade. It is therefore logical to begin small and build toward your most convincing argument. When you borrow money from your parents, you mention how responsible you've been recently, your good grades last semester, and other things that set the stage. But your big persuasions — your safe driving record, your plan to fill the car with gas, how desperately you need it — come at the end. You don't start big then fade; you tuck in any tenuous ideas early on and save up for the grand finale.

The same principle applies to writing. The writer of the essay on Bruce Springsteen looks over the four ideas: songs, biography, Freehold cause, and the state song proposal. She decides which she has the most to say about and then revises her ideas, regroups, and builds her argument toward the most persuasive point. The final plan might look something like this:

Thesis: Bruce Springsteen belongs to New Jersey

1. Biographical proof
    a. born in New Jersey
    b. lives in New Jersey

2. Involved with New Jersey
    a. a Springsteen song was proposed as a state song for New Jersey
    b. Freehold workers' cause
3. His music is inspired by New Jersey
    a. "Jungleland"
    b. "Jersey Girl"
    c. "Atlantic City"
    d. "4th of July, Asbury Park"
    e. "My Hometown"

Since there were five separate examples for the paragraph about songs, and only two points to be made in the other paragraphs, an order of importance dictates that the song paragraph be last.

This organizing process is not a substitute for the final outline you need for a 15-page research paper; but it is an adequate preparation for most short essays or essay test answers and a necessary first step if such a final outline is required.

Getting the Most Out of Prewriting

The prewriting process can take you from the bewilderment of having just received an assignment to confidence in being ready to write. Use it as much as you need. You may brainstorm and organize a test answer in a total of five minutes, or mull over ideas for weeks, brainstorm three or four times, and then sit down and compose a final outline. Most writers need some help and preparation; they gather their ideas together in a *brainstorm*, sort and *group* them, *focus* on a tentative thesis, and then *organize* their proof in a logical pattern.

Drafting

The next step is to begin writing. Complete the research and rereading of sources; continue to refine, add to, and regroup your ideas. Then begin to write your essay in these three parts:

Introduction
Body
Conclusion

Although the three parts work together, they need to be thought of separately. The introduction and conclusion are necessary frames for the real substance of your essay, the body. Like the bread in a sandwich, the introduction and conclusion keep everything neat, organized, and together. In between lies the important business, the evidence or proof itself. All three parts make the whole.

The Introduction

There are essentially two strategies for an introduction. One is to provide the reader with a road map for the area about to be covered. This is especially helpful if the territory is tricky or the journey is long, as with a complex or extensive essay. The underlying principle is to provide the reader with a sort of outline of the essay's content.

THE ROAD-MAP INTRODUCTION

> Thesis (main idea)
> Reference to each *major* point of the essay
> A concluding sentence that returns, in different words, to the thesis

Here is an example of this type of introduction for an essay on the novels of Charles Dickens:

> Dickens' novels often present children as the adults or "parents" in their families. In early works like *Nicholas Nickleby,* the real parents are basically unreliable. The children cannot count on them for support, guidance, or love. But the problem intensifies in works like *Bleak House* where adults often act like children. In Dickens' last completed novel, *Our Mutual Friend,* Jenny Wren and Lizzie Hexam suggest the final extension of this theme: they are mothers to their own fathers. Throughout Dickens' works it is the children who run things and hold the families together, while the adults fantasize, dream, or drink.

This introduction does not actually discuss the examples or prove the point of the essay, but it leaves no doubt as to what will be discussed and in what order. It names the thesis, outlines the three supporting points that will be treated (*Nicholas Nickleby, Bleak House,* and *Our Mutual Friend*), and allows the reader to see the general plan of the whole essay.

THE GENERAL-TO-SPECIFIC INTRODUCTION

The other type of introduction does not outline the paper. Instead, it draws the reader into the topic slowly, leaving the presentation of individual points to the body of the essay:

> A general statement (in the topic area)
> More specific statements that lead to thesis
> Thesis (main idea)

Here is an example of this type of introduction for the same paper on Charles Dickens:

> The nineteenth century took the family seriously. Queen Victoria and Prince Albert were a model family, the parents of nine children. And in the novels that were meant to be read to the family group, family connections and relationships were major themes. Charles Dickens felt the presence of these themes and, as the unhappily married father of ten children, knew what family life was like. His novels, however, often present the family in a rather inverted manner. The children act as parents to childish adults.

This introduction slowly defines the areas to be discussed and gradually brings the reader to the topic. The sample begins with the nineteenth century and nineteenth-century families, then goes on to Dickens' own family, and finally to the families in Dickens' novels. The actual novels are not named, but the topic is clearly defined in the last sentence.

This type of introduction is remarkably flexible. It can be brief or lengthy. The opening can be many things; for example, background information, a few words about the author and the time period, begin this essay. (See Sample 2 in Chapter 6 for a college essay that uses this type of introduction.) A definition could also have been used. A science paper on eating habits might want to define "eating" in a broader sense than usual in order to discuss ingestive behaviors in one-celled organisms. This type of introduction could also begin with a common assumption and then contradict it:

> Jobs are scarce. Unemployment is up and people are holding on to whatever jobs they have. There's not much movement in major corporations and, when people retire or depart, their work is absorbed by the survivors. Yet this may be the best time in the last ten years to look for a new job.

Newspapers and magazines like *Time* and *Newsweek* often use this introduction strategy, capturing the reader's attention with a brief story or incident:

> The hot night of July 26, 1985 threatened a thunderstorm in Henderson, Texas. When Nancy-Jean Alberts went out to empty the trash, she noticed the sky was dark for 8 p.m. and lines of heat lightning darted along the horizon.

This article might turn out to be about a murder, a flood, or even trash. The narration at the beginning has caught the readers' attention and drawn them into the paragraph; a forceful and focused thesis statement will follow.

The general-to-specific introduction is flexible and simple. You have some choices in its construction and do not have to give away all your ideas in the first paragraph. It is suitable for most essays and is especially useful for those in a timed situation when you may not know at the beginning exactly what points (or how many) you will cover. The only pitfall is the first sentence — do not make it overly general. "Life is interesting" doesn't sound very interesting and would require a very lengthy paragraph to narrow it down adequately to a thesis. "Shakespeare is a great playwright" is certainly more specific, but it lacks impact. Don't let the first sentence grab the reader too vigorously, either. An attention-getter is a good idea but it can be overused or overdone. Remember your audience and let it dictate your tone. You don't want to begin:

> Wha-a-a-a-a-a! Who's that howling in *Bleak House?* Is it a crying baby or is it simply Mr. Skimpole?

Make the first sentence interesting and related to the thesis but try to engage the reader's interest without being confusing or shocking.

IS AN INTRODUCTION ABSOLUTELY NECESSARY?

Most essays need a paragraph of some length to identify the topic and get things going, but there are a few exceptions. A short essay (one or two paragraphs) does not need an introduction. A few sentences at the beginning of the first paragraph can make the topic clear. Some tests and examinations (and some college application essays) provide only a few minutes or a few inches for your responses. In such a case, a full introduction would waste precious time and space. If you are given an essay test with several questions, do not fret over the introduction for a *15-point* question, "To what extent did Metternich influence diplomacy in the nineteenth century?" Begin with one or two sentences drawn from the question itself (you might simply state that Metternich *did* change diplomatic techniques) and give the rest of the allotted time and space to the *proof*.

Another time to consider omitting the introduction is in an inductive essay. This essay takes the reader through a discussion without a clear focus, revealing its intention only at the end. This is a suspenseful and creative approach to the essay and can be very effective. But, it is best reserved for less stressful situations than the college essay, for the most able writers, and for short, creative topics.

Finally, a narrative essay might survive without an introduction. The writer tells a story, recounts a series of incidents, and then draws meaning from them in the conclusion. Like the inductive essay, this format requires readers to go some distance on faith. They aren't sure to what they ought to be paying attention, but finally, it all makes sense in the conclusion. (Sample 3 in Chapter 6 uses something like this strategy.) This strategy can make a very effective *short* college essay, but remember, it puts a significant burden on the reader and is best reserved for occasional use.

Most of the time, you'll want an introduction and most often either the road-map or the general-to-specific format will give your essay a strong start and a clear direction.

The Body

The substance of your essay is the body. Bound in place by the introduction and the conclusion, the body does the work of the essay: It proves. It presents the evidence that will convert the reader to your opinion. Each paragraph of the body is a block of proof, a chunk of evidence of the validity of your thesis, and each is developed from one aspect or point of your thesis, as sketched out in the simple outline.

The Shakespeare essay, for example, uses three plays as examples to prove that Shakespeare was concerned with the restoration of order. The outline gives three subtopics: order in *Romeo and Juliet*, in *The Taming of the Shrew*, and in *Hamlet*. Thus, you plan three paragraphs for the body, one for each play. If, however, in drafting the essay you discover new aspects of the topic that should be mentioned — perhaps that *Hamlet* is a play about both the proper order in a kingdom and also about one man's drive for personal order and revenge for the death of his father — the plan can be expanded and the number of paragraphs in the body adjusted, in this case, to four, one for each play and two for *Hamlet.*

The important thing is to prove, with specific and vivid detail, the correctness of your view. You must present a sequence of *arguments* for your thesis rather than plot summaries, story outlines, or a review of the course of history thus far.

Selection is the key. You must go through each part of your argument and select the scenes, details, quotations, and facts that show the truth of your view. To substantiate your thesis, you must bring to the reader's attention only that evidence that cumulatively shows that you are correct. Select. Do not retell! It is not persuasive to retell a whole story, review every event of a war, or summarize everything that has been said on your topic. Your essay should be based on your angle of vision, your special lens, your way of looking at a larger complex of ideas. And in support of your thesis, you need to gather *only* those points or ideas that prove your view is right.

Each paragraph of the body should conform to this pattern (or vary from it for a *good* reason):

TOPIC SENTENCE
(the main idea of this paragraph and its relation to the thesis)

DEVELOPMENT
(the evidence — events, facts, statistics, reasons, examples, details, things said in the literature, things said about the literature — presented in some logical order)

CLINCHER
(especially useful in a long or complex paragraph)

Topic Sentences

The topic sentence is important in two ways: it identifies the subject of the paragraph, and it shows how the paragraph is connected to the thesis. It may even form a transition from the previous paragraph.

1. thesis	Shakespeare explored the instability of life and the
2. transition	need for order not only in a comic setting but also
3. topic	in the tragic circumstances of Prince Hamlet.
1. topic	But things get worse in *Our Mutual Friend.*
2. transition	Now parents and adults are not just silly and
3. thesis	irresponsible; they are the children of the families.

In the first example, the writer reiterates, in slightly different words, the main thesis of the essay, mentions the point of the previous paragraph (a comedy's treatment of this theme), and then establishes what this paragraph will discuss (*Hamlet*). In the second instance, the writer uses two sentences to get going: the first names the paragraph's topic (*Our Mutual Friend*); the second fits that topic into the larger scheme of the thesis (irresponsibility and childish adults).

There is, and always should be, flexibility in a format. Every paragraph does not have to begin with a reference to the preceding paragraph. A topic sentence doesn't have to be first in a paragraph, either. But each sentence that appears before the topic sentence runs the risk of being wasted. Your readers don't yet know what's going on, and may lose interest or the sense of continuity. They ask, "Why am I reading this?" It is therefore helpful if each paragraph declares, and usually the sooner the better, its topic and how it intends to support it.

Development

The middle of each paragraph is the support. It is a combination of facts, events, quotations, examples, and reasons that proves the point of that paragraph and, in so doing, proves the thesis of the essay. It is the evidence that will persuade your reader. Notice the combination of different types of support in this paragraph from an essay about insanity in *Moby Dick*:

> Another way Melville makes the reader aware of the
> transition from sanity to insanity is in his imagery.
> Throughout the novel, he weaves a careful pattern of
> images that turn from normal to abnormal, from
> familiar to strange. For example, the images of fire EXAMPLE
> begin in the friendly inns of Nantucket and New
> Bedford. Ishmael rejoices in the privilege of "making
> my own summer with my own coals" (p. 61). Fire is QUOTATION
> here warmth and companionship. Even Queequeg's
> EVENT sacrificial fire to Yojo serves as the beginning of inti-
> mate friendship between the two sailors. But slowly
> this begins to change. By the middle of the novel, fire
> begins to suggest evil. It is associated with Ahab's mad CRITIC'S QUOTATION
> purpose, what Richard Chase calls "the self-absorption
> that leads to isolation, madness and suicide" (*The
> American Novel and Its Tradition*, p. 109). Ahab calls
> QUOTATION himself a volcano in "The Quarter-Deck" chapter and
> the crew swears death to Moby Dick in a fiery crossing EVENT
> of harpoons. Later, in the chapter called "The Try-
> works," Ishmael compares the rendering fires to the DETAIL
> fires of hell. By Chapter 113, hot-forged harpoons are
> being dipped in blood as Ahab baptizes the crew "*in* EVENT
> QUOTATION *nomine diabolis*" (p. 373). Nature's fire, lightning,
> warns the crew away by igniting the masts and nearly
> striking Ahab. The happy homefires of Nantucket have
> EVENTS changed into the dangerous fires of Ahab's mad pas-
> sion; thus they reinforce the novel's movement from
> sanity to insanity.
>
> Like Melville's imagery, his characters move toward madness. First there is Pip . . . .

Remember to follow a logical order in the presentation of the body's paragraphs. Chronological order or order of location have been mentioned as possible types of organization. Another excellent choice is order of importance, beginning with your minor points and building toward your most important argument at the end.

Clincher

At the end of the paragraph, a sentence often appears that summarizes the whole paragraph and refocuses on the essay's thesis. Because this sentence may echo the topic sentence, student writers often wonder if their papers aren't getting repetitious. "Isn't it awfully boring to say this one thing at the beginning and end of the paper, and at the beginning and end of every paragraph, too?" Remember, however, that you are covering ideas familiar and clear only to you. You must make them equally clear to readers who have never thought exactly this way about this topic. They have to be led a little. There has to be repetition. Each topic sentence should sound somewhat alike and relate to the thesis. The concluding sentences of some, or all, of the body paragraphs will return to the main idea of the essay. There will be changes in wording and perhaps only the repetition of a key word (like "order" in the Shakespeare essay) to remind readers of what's happening. But don't think you're helping them by retelling the plot. Provide signs, repetitions, along the way to keep readers on *your path.* The end of the paragraph about Moby Dick is a good example of this kind of helpful repetition.

A short or simple paragraph, or one that appears right before the conclusion, does not need the summary sentence at the end. You can draw the paragraph to a close in some other way, perhaps by simply adding a sentence that makes it clear the paragraph is complete.

Points to Remember

The body of the essay is its most important part. You marshall all the evidence you can find to support your theory and present it in a series of paragraphs designed to convince your readers. Most of these paragraphs will begin with a topic sentence that connects the paragraph to the thesis. All of them will be made up of facts, examples, and extensive specific support for your point. Many will end with the summarizing clincher that redirects the reader's attention to the thesis. The repetitions of the thesis and its rewording in topic sentences and clinchers aren't useless reiterations; they are the necessary coherence that creates the focus. The body should be by far the greatest percentage of the essay for it is there that the essay will win its argument.

Patterns are useful. Good tailors begin with standard patterns and soon develop their own. So it is with writers. The idea is to begin with rules and use them where appropriate. There is no reason why you can't "break" a rule as long as you have a reason and are doing so consciously. The goal of any writing advice is to help writers be more aware and in control of their material, and to avoid writing with no idea of what they should do or why they are at one point succeeding and at another failing. More than any student comment, "She didn't like my paper" is the one that drives me crazy. I have never graded a paper on whether I liked it or not. I have always determined a grade according to how successful the student was in organizing the material and in validating his or her argument. The paper made its own grade.

Finally, keep in mind that there is no secret set of "right" answers stashed in the school safe. The purpose of an essay is not to guess what the teacher believes about a topic and win an A; it is to develop a good thesis and prove it. Critical opinion changes, even among the leaders in a given field. Notice the ups and downs that the reputations of presidents suffer. Consider the esteem with which Hemingway was regarded in the 1950s versus the respect awarded him in the feminist age. To paraphrase Emerson's favorite quotation, "Ask for no man's opinion but your own." Every age must write its own criticism. So the essay is not about latching onto THE ONE RIGHT ANSWER. It is about your ability to find a possible answer and to make a convincing argument for it.

This is especially true for the college essay. Many students set out to "tell them what they want to hear." This is a fruitless and contradictory goal. What the essay should provide is a sense of you, a concrete and specific view with the facts to back it up (prove it).

An interesting idea with no evidence is a pointless exercise in creativity; a lot of plot review or a collection of facts without a focus is merely exposition. Think of two opposing lawyers; each has the same events and facts to work with yet the prosecutor selects and presents them so the accused looks like a cold-blooded murderer while the attorney for the defense selects and presents them so that the client seems as innocent as an angel. Every essay needs a good thesis and a focused selection of supporting material to make it clear and convincing.

Do not wander off this straight and narrow path to either side: to the "let's-tell-'em-what-they-want-to-hear" essay that presents a razzle-dazzle idea with no evidence, or to the "let's-tell-'em-all-we-know-and-hope-for-the-best" (travelog/autobiography) essay that is full of facts with no focus. In any essay (and especially in the college essay), you need both *focus* and *proof.*

A Special Organizational Problem

THE COMPARATIVE ESSAY

The comparative essay is a special assignment. It is a challenging format that is often used for Advanced Placement test questions and final examination topics. The organization is not difficult as long as you keep in mind the comparative purpose of the paper. The pitfall is writing a comparative essay that never does any comparing — lots of information with no comparisons drawn between the points. A history student, for example, asked to compare the programs set up to regulate business that were passed in the administration of Woodrow Wilson with those passed in the administration of Franklin D. Roosevelt, might recount all she knows about Wilson, then all she knows about Roosevelt, and then conclude. This is not a comparison.

One way to get it right is to discuss the first item of the comparison, in this case Wilson's regulatory programs, then discuss the second item in the same order used in the previous paragraph and with *constant reference* to what has *already* been said about Wilson. The second paragraph will include sentences such as the following ones.

> "Roosevelt had opposition similar to that confronted by Wilson, but he employed different tactics to overcome it . . . ," or
>
> "But like Wilson, Roosevelt found his backers were fickle . . . . ," or
>
> "These measures finally were more successful than what Wilson accomplished . . . ."

Proceed in sequence through your points, sticking with the order established in the first paragraph of the body, continually making comparative comments about the similarities and differences of each new point to what has already been discussed. The conclusion for this essay should summarize fully and methodically all the comparisons that you have discussed in the essay.

Another method of organization, more likely to be used in an essay prepared outside of class than for an examination question, separates aspects of the comparison. In the example given above, the writer would isolate individual aspects of the topic — creation of programs, implementation, obstacles, success, impact —

and then look at each president's handling of them. Here is a pair of outlines that shows the difference between the two ways of writing a comparison:

A. COMPARING WILSON AND FDR

1. Wilson
    a. programs
    b. implementation
    c. obstacles
    d. success
    e. impact
2. FDR (with reference to Wilson)
    a. programs
    b. implementation
    c. obstacles
    d. success
    e. impact
3. Comparative summary

B. COMPARING WILSON AND FDR

1. Creation of programs
    a. Wilson
    b. FDR
2. Implementation
    a. Wilson
    b. FDR
3. Obstacles
    a. Wilson
    b. FDR
4. Success
    a. Wilson
    b. FDR
5. Long-term impact
    a. Wilson
    b. FDR
6. Short conclusion

The second way does not necessarily cover more material than the first, but it is more directly comparative and clearly organized. The reader can follow the comparisons more easily, and the conclusion doesn't have to do as much. Like a lot of things in life, the second way is harder . . . but better!

The Conclusion

The conclusion can serve one or two functions. It should refocus the readers' attention on the main idea of the essay, remind them of what they have just read, and reaffirm the validity of the author's argument. This is the summary conclusion and, although not particularly creative, it gets the job done. The format is:

> Thesis (slightly reworded)
> Reference to the major points of the body (in order)
> Clincher

A more creative use of the conclusion is as a springboard for a new idea. After refocusing and briefly summarizing, the writer goes on to judge, speculate, generalize, or recommend.

> Thesis (slightly reworded)
> Short summary of the essay
> Additional idea that grows logically from what has been proven in the essay

This type of conclusion does not suit every topic, as there will be times when you do not have anything to add to the end of your essay. But, there are many times when it can work for you. Here are four examples:

1. The essay on Shakespeare's theme of order might end with a generalization about Elizabethan England and the order that people in that time saw throughout their world. You would thus connect this particular theme from three of Shakespeare's plays to larger trends and ideas of his age.
2. An essay on the athletic facilities at your school in which you urge the creation of an all-weather track might recommend the creation of a capital fund campaign to raise the money needed for the project. The essay itself would only show the need and value of the track. Having reiterated those ideas in the conclusion, you could go on to suggest how the work might get done.

3. An essay on a gerbil experiment might speculate on other possible parallel experiments that could be performed or recommend further studies.

4. A college essay describing an applicant might use the conclusion to connect goals and personal qualities to the college itself. For example, if you have proven you are a science buff, in your conclusion you might show why MIT is the logical choice for you. (See Sample 1 in Chapter 6.)

To determine whether this type of conclusion is appropriate, at the end of your essay ask yourself, "So what? What does all that I've proven mean? Where can I go from here?" If there isn't any real answer to this, then sum up and stop. But if a suggestion or generalization comes to mind, you might use it for a "springboard" conclusion. This conclusion is especially useful for assigned essay topics that request the writer to discuss two unequal ideas. For example, a history teacher might ask: "To what extent did the role of women in society change during the 1930s? Do you see any parallels to your own situation today?" The real heart of this question is the role of women in the 1930s. An additional, although less important, part of the question asks the student to assess her life in terms of what she has already said about the 1930s. The student constructs an essay with individual paragraphs devoted to areas of change concerning women: the domestic scene, the job market, economic power, fashion. The conclusion might sum up these points and then go on to comment on the writer's own situation. Since this is a lesser part of the question, it could be adequately treated as the final aspect of a conclusion. Judgments and comparisons could be based on what has already been said in the body.

This second type of conclusion would not be a good choice if the question asked for the discussion of two *equal* points: "Discuss the forces that created the League of Nations and those that destroyed it." Here, the best bet is a body divided into two sections, one on creation and one on destruction. The conclusion would then merely summarize what was presented in the body.

As you plan and write the essay, you will see how much you have to say, how important are the various parts of the essay, how to structure the paragraphs themselves, how much repetition is needed. You will choose an introduction that suits your topic, create body paragraphs in support of your thesis, and select an appropriate conclusion.

Transition

Everyone who has watched the television program "Wild Kingdom" over the years knows about transition. The host always creates strong transitions between the show and the commercials:

> That lion cub was almost eaten by those jackals. But luckily his father was there to protect him. You'll feel that same security when you're protected by (sponsor's name) insurance.

By repeating a key word (like "protect") and using demonstratives (that, those) and transitional expressions (like "same"), viewers are encouraged to see a connection between the program and the advertisers.

Transition is the most important stylistic skill you can master. It is the way to create connections and coherence in your writing. It is absolutely essential to a smooth introduction, important within and especially at the beginning of body paragraphs, and helpful as you move into the conclusion.

There are three major ways to create transition:

RULE 1

Use transitional expressions. These words and phrases make connections wherever they appear:

To show time or sequence: first, second, then
To show cause: therefore, thus, hence
To show similarity: and, like, similarly, likewise
To show difference: on the other hand, however

Example: Ahab sees Moby Dick as his goal in life. *Likewise*, Jay Gatsby sees Daisy as his goal.

RULE 2

Repeat key words and sentence structure (parallelism).

Example: Ahab *sees* Moby Dick *as his goal* in life. Likewise, Jay Gatsby *sees* Daisy *as his goal.* (Note the repetition of the words "sees" and "goal" and the use of parallel sentence structure.)

Example: ". . . that government of the *people*, by the *people*, for the *people*, shall not perish from the earth." ("People" is repeated in a series of three prepositional phrases.)

RULE 3

Use pronouns (he, she, it, they) and demonstrative nouns and adjectives (this, that).

Example: Francis Bacon: He that hath wife and children hath given hostages to fortune; for *they* are impediments to great enterprise . . . ."

Example: Franklin D. Roosevelt: "The New Deal is our hope. *It* is the way to recovery. *It* is the immediate way. *It* is the strongest assurance that the recovery will endure."

The following paragraph relies heavily on transition to guide the reader. Notice the different methods used, particularly the paragraph hook that connects this paragraph to the one that follows.

> Another way Melville makes the reader aware of the transition from sanity to insanity is in his imagery. Throughout the novel, he weaves a careful pattern of images that turn from normal to abnormal, from familiar to strange. For example, the images of fire

WORD REPETITIC

begin in the friendly inns of Nantucket and New Bedford. Ishmael rejoices in the privilege of "making my own summer with my own coals" (p. 61). Fire is here warmth and companionship. Even Queequeg's sacrificial fire to Yojo serves as the beginning of intimate friendship between the two sailors. But slowly this begins to change. By the middle of the novel, fire begins to suggest evil. It is associated with Ahab's mad purpose, what Richard Chase calls "the self-absorption that leads to isolation, madness and suicide" (*The American Novel and Its Tradition*, p. 109). Ahab calls himself a volcano in "The Quarter-Deck" chapter and the crew swears death to Moby Dick in a fiery crossing of harpoons. Later, in the chapter called "The Try-works," Ishmael compares the rendering fires to the fires of hell. By Chapter 113, hot-forged harpoons are being dipped in blood as Ahab baptizes the crew "*in nomine diabolis*" (p. 373). Nature's fire, lightning, warns the crew away by igniting the masts and nearly striking Ahab. The happy homefires of Nantucket have changed into the dangerous fires of Ahab's mad passion; thus they reinforce the novel's movement from sanity to insanity.

TRANSITIONAL EXPRESSION

PRONOUN

Like Melville's imagery, his characters move toward madness. First there is Pip. . . .

PARAGRAPH HOOK

Try to keep transition in mind as you draft and especially as you revise your essay. It will provide the flow and cohesiveness that every essay needs.

Editing

The final stage of the essay process is editing. Proofread your essay carefully and slowly; read it aloud. Look for:

FOCUS: Check for coherence throughout the essay so that the reader can find the main idea (thesis) and follow it from beginning to end. You might have someone read just your introduction to see what he or she thinks your essay is about. If there's any doubt in the reader's mind, keep rewriting that paragraph. Also be sure your main idea is not only clear in your introduction but is referred to *throughout* the essay, especially at the beginning of body paragraphs.

PROOF: Be sure the development of each body paragraph is extensive, specific, and clearly related to your main point. This is the meat of the sandwich — make it substantial.

CORRECTNESS: Check your spelling (or use a spelling checker on your computer). Even for some very bright people, spelling is always a problem. Find a good dictionary and check every word you're unsure of: don't be lazy about spelling. I know a recruiter who turned down a good job candidate because he hadn't bothered to spell the company name properly in his application letter. "He's careless; he'll only cause headaches for me and hassles and embarrassment at the top." Right or wrong, we are often judged on small things.

In a second reading, try to pay attention to *how* things are said, as well as to what you have said. Try to read with the eyes of an enemy looking for problems, keeping the following in mind:

1. A simple style is best. Good writing sounds like speech rather than a vocabulary review lesson. Where you are having problems expressing an idea, try using shorter sentences and simpler words rather than longer sentences and a thesaurus.
2. Evaluate your writing for sentence variety. Write some long, complex sentences; use a short sentence once in a while for impact. Don't begin all your sentences with the subject or with the same word.
3. Remember your audience and the requirements of the assignment. There are differences in the structure, style, and precision required in a science journal and in a finished lab report, in an essay for your drama class and in a final term paper in a Shakespeare seminar for senior English majors only.

4. As in everything, there are usage conventions and somewhat arbitrary rules of formality. Most academic writing requires that you observe these conventions, although each audience will be a little different and each teacher may have his or her own pet peeves. Usually these are explained early in a course or described in the writing handbook recommended by the teacher. In general:
   - Avoid dashes and exclamation points. They are the junk food of the punctuation world, just as the semicolon is the truffle. The former are too casual for the tone of most essays; the latter is best used sparingly.
   - Avoid parentheses; most often the sentence merely needs reorganization.
   - Avoid asking questions. An essay should answer questions; asking them is contrived, since you intend to answer them yourself.
   - Avoid setting off expressions that are wrong to begin with in sanitizing quotation marks. "Monet was really 'into' water lilies" is not appropriate; don't try to get away with it by putting "into" in quotation marks. Omit the offending word and state the information in a different way: "Monet found water lilies fascinating."
   - Avoid contractions, abbreviations, and slang; keep your style both reasonably formal and scrupulously correct.

Set the essay aside for a few days — unless it's due tomorrow! If it is, take this moment to resolve *not* to wait until the last minute next time.

When you think you are ready to look at your essay with a fresh, objective eye, go back, reread it, and make any changes that will improve the final draft. Once you are satisfied, it is time for a little outside evaluation. Ask someone whose writing ability you respect to read your essay. The writing center at your school is a good option. Try to pick a reader whose comments aren't threatening to you so you can really hear what he or she is saying. Your boyfriend or girlfriend is probably not the best choice.

Ultimately, you are the best editor. No one can speak for you; your own words and ideas are your best bet. Be sure to proofread the final draft several times yourself to eliminate all errors in spelling, punctuation, and grammar. Errors are distracting and undermine the points you are making, so proofread, proofread, proofread!

Understanding and Avoiding Plagiarism

You've heard the word *plagiarism* but may not know precisely what it means. Taking someone else's words or ideas and presenting them as your own is a form of stealing called plagiarism. Quotations from *Hamlet* in a paper on *Hamlet* are the support for your theory. Words and ideas from critics who agree with you add credibility to your argument, whether you quote them directly or paraphrase their words. But you must always give credit where credit is due. Identify in the text or by footnotes all direct quotations, paraphrases, and borrowed ideas. It doesn't matter whether the source is today's newspaper, an old out-of-print book, or a friend's research report; you must acknowledge the use of any borrowed material.

Reviewing the Process

Summary

The Essay: The written defense of an opinion
The Introduction
  The Road-Map Introduction
    Thesis
    Major Points
    Clincher
  The General-to-Specific Introduction
    A General Statement in the Topic Area

Increasingly Specific Statements
Thesis
The Body
A Sample Body Paragraph
Topic Sentence (states topic of paragraph, shows relation of paragraph to thesis, may show transition from the previous paragraph)
Development (extensive specific examples and evidence to support your point . . . about 80 percent of the paragraph)
Clincher
The Conclusion
Summary Conclusion
Thesis
Major Points
Clincher
Speculative Conclusion
Thesis
Short Summary of Essay
New Point (generalization, speculation, judgment, recommendation)

The essay is a marvelously flexible form. Its only strict requirements are a clear and continual focus and plenty of proof. "Tell 'em what you're gonna tell 'em, tell 'em, tell 'em what you told 'em." Use a beginning to present your thesis, a middle full of persuasive evidence, and an end that returns to and reaffirms the thesis.

The process begins with the gathering of ideas by brainstorming, a process which should result in a specific thesis and a simple outline. This can take three minutes during a final examination or several weeks in the preparation of a research paper. Depending on the length and complexity of the topic, you may or may not want to refine and expand the simple outline as you continue to plan, research, and prepare.

Once you're writing, create an introduction that makes your thesis clear. The introduction can also make your whole essay plan clear. The body is the proof, and should be a careful selection of points that validate your thesis. A conclusion at the end should sum up what you've said or raise further possibilities.

Keep your style simple and stress transition between ideas and between paragraphs.

Edit your work yourself and with some outside help. You will probably want to consult a writing handbook for the fine points of style, grammar, research, and footnoting. Check the Suggested Reading list in the back of this book for the names of some helpful reference books. Make a final copy of your essay, proofread it three times, and feel satisfied at having followed a process through from beginning to end.

Remember that the advice in this chapter is not intended to be an inflexible set of do's and don'ts for writing. These are suggestions, beginnings; some you will always use, some you will outgrow. All are designed to put you in control of your own writing.

4

What's the Question?

> Two roads diverged in a yellow wood,
> And sorry I could not travel both
> And be one traveler, long I stood
> And looked down one as far as I could
> To where it bent in the undergrowth;
>
> Then took the other, as just as fair . . . .
>
> *from "The Road Not Taken" by Robert Frost*

We define ourselves by our choices. The big ones shape our lives: what path to take, what career, who to marry, where to live. But even small choices are self-defining: Do you prefer the top half of the bagel or the bottom? Billy Joel or Twisted Sister? J. D. Salinger or Stephen King? BASIC or PASCAL? Colleges believe that by observing the process of choosing, they gain insight into the applicant, so most application essays are experiments in choice. *How* you write the essay will reveal your writing abilities. *What* you write about will reveal you.

Here is a sampling of the application essay policies of a wide variety of colleges and universities — small private and selective institutions and large state colleges. Remember, the small and selective colleges that maintain a more personal admissions process are more likely to require one or two essays. They rate the essay as a major piece in the puzzle. But even large colleges and universities like Brigham Young, Michigan State, Tulane, and the University of Southern California suggest or require an essay, and turn to it for additional insight, in special situations, or to settle "gray zone" applications.

Colleges and Their Questions

COLLEGE OR UNIVERSITY	*NUMBER OF ESSAYS REQUIRED*	*TYPE OF QUESTION**	*NUMBER OF PARAGRAPH QUESTIONS*
Alfred University	1	1	1
Amherst College	2	3; 2 or 6	3
Arizona State University	0		0
Bennington College	1	2	2
Bentley College	2	4; 2	0
Boston University	2 of 6	1, 2, 5, 6, 7, 9	1
Bowdoin College	1 of 3	1, 8, other	0
Brigham Young University	1	4	0
Brandeis University	1	2	0
Bryn Mawr College	1 of 4	1, 10, 11, 12	2
Bucknell University	1 of 3	2, 6, 7	0
Columbia University	1	1	3
Common Application (used by 116 colleges)	1 of 3	2, 6, 7	1

*Numbers correspond to the following types of essays which are described in more detail in this chapter.

1. A personal statement
2. Describe a significant interest or experience
3. How have you grown and developed
4. Why have you selected College X
5. Why have you chosen this career or profession
6. The national issue question
7. The famous person question
8. The hero question
9. The speech or article
10. The book question
11. The challenge question
12. Your high school curriculum
13. Good advice
14. Quotations
15. The invention question

Other indicates a type of essay that does not fit any of the categories defined above.

COLLEGE OR UNIVERSITY	*NUMBER OF ESSAYS REQUIRED*	*TYPE OF QUESTION*	*NUMBER OF PARAGRAPH QUESTIONS*
Dartmouth College	2	10, 11, 13; create your own	3
DePauw University	1 of 4	5, 8, 10, 11	0
Duke University	1	1	2
Emory University	2 of 3	14	0
Fairleigh Dickinson University	0	optional statement	2
Georgetown University	1 of 2 or 2	1, 4, 5	1
George Washington University	0		2
Glassboro State College	1	4	0
Goucher College	1 of 4	1, 10, 15, other	0
Hamilton College	1 of 4	2, 6, 10, 11, plus writing sample	3
Harvard University	1	1	5
Illinois Institute of Technology	1	4	0
Johns Hopkins University	1	5	0
Lenoir-Rhyne College	1 of 3	1, 4, 6	0
Mansfield University of Pennsylvania	0		0
Marist College	0		1
Michigan State University	0	optional statement	0
Middlebury College	1	4	0
Monmouth College, New Jersey	0		0
Monmouth College, Illinois	0		1
Moravian College	0		0
New Jersey Institute of Technology	0		1
Northwestern University	1	1, 2, 3, 11	2
Ogelthorpe University	0		0
Pace University	1	3, 6, plus writing sample	1
Pennsylvania State University	0		0
Pepperdine University	1	1 plus writing sample	2

COLLEGE OR UNIVERSITY	*NUMBER OF ESSAYS REQUIRED*	*TYPE OF QUESTION*	*NUMBER OF PARAGRAPH QUESTIONS*
Polytechnic Institute of New York	0		0
Princeton University	3	1, 2, 2	2
Providence College	1	2	0
Rutgers University	0		0
Seton Hall University	0	optional statement	0
Simmons College	1	2, 4, 13	0
Sweet Briar College	1	1	2
Trenton State College	0		1
Trinity College (Connecticut)	3	6, 9, 13	0
Tufts University	1	1	0
Tulane University	1	1	0
University of Delaware	0		0
University of Maine	1	5	0
University of Michigan	1	1	0
University of Nevada	0		0
University of Pennsylvania	1 of 3	7, 13, other	0
University of Richmond	1 of 3	2, 6, 7	0
University of Rochester	0		0
University of South Carolina	1	4	0
University of Vermont	0		2
Vassar College	1 of 3	2, 15, other	0
Wesleyan University	2	8, 1	2
Williams College	1	2	0
William Smith College	1	2	0
Yale University	2	2, 1	0

The applications have a variety of areas that need more than one-word answers. Not all of these are actually essays. So to begin with, make a list of all the questions you have to answer for your applications. There will be a duplication of questions and you may be able to recycle some of your answers with minimal changes. Schools that accept the Common Application (there are 116 of them) make life a little easier. And various wordings of the question "Describe yourself" or "Write an essay that gives a sense of you as an individual" appear on many applications.

Don't, however, plan to use the same answer for two entirely different questions. Carol Lunkenheimer, at Northwestern, warns: "We can recognize Stanford's or Dartmouth's question. We want an applicant who cares enough about Northwestern to write an original essay for *our* application." And don't use your answer to "What influenced your decision to apply to Lenoir-Rhyne?" for "Why are you interested in attending Trinity?" There will probably be some similarities in course offerings, programs, location, or philosophy among the colleges you apply to, but the "Why us?" questions need answers tailored to each individual school.

Once you've sketched out what you have to do, you can see that your answers will vary in length. Some questions provide an inch or two for the answer; some give a full page with the offer of additional sheets if needed. Stick as closely as possible to the space provided. The college is suggesting how extensive and complex an answer they want by how much paper they supply. Let that be your guideline. Don't fall too short or go much beyond the limit. Readers are assigned many folders to evaluate and are not perusing your application at their leisure. Make your answers *very legible* and to the point. In all likelihood, three or four pages in a crabbed, bunched-up scribble will be skimmed; you'll get more attention with a concise, typed performance.

Short-Answer Questions

The real difference between the questions is the issue of choice. Some questions ask for a simple list of activities, summer work, jobs, honors, or recent reading. These questions are not difficult and do not require soul-searching. Some schools even ask for this information in the form of a chart. The simple résumé you created for your guidance counselor or your recommending teacher will help with these descriptive questions.

As a List

List the items chronologically from most recent to most remote, or from most important to least. Provide complete information and follow the same format for each item:

June-August 1985	Lifeguard Springfield Town Pool 40 hours per week $4.00 per hour
June-August 1984	Swimming instructor Springfield Day Camp 20 hours per week $3.50 per hour

In Paragraph Form

Include the activity, your involvement, and the time commitment. Be sure to clarify names of groups or titles since *The Mirror* or Key Club by themselves are not clear to admissions personnel. As one admissions staffer put it, "At some schools the Spanish Club is just a bunch of kids who get together on Friday nights for tacos." Make it clear that your activities have involved responsibility and effort.

1. I am now president of the Book Worms, a school club that does volunteer work for the town library. Each month I attend one two-hour planning meeting with the library staff and schedule time slots and assignments for the 11 other club members; I work at the reference desk from 7 to 9 p.m. every Tuesday night.
2. During my junior year, I was assistant sports editor for *The Mirror*, our monthly school newspaper. I wrote at least one story for each monthly issue and edited one or two articles by the junior high sportswriter for each issue.

Don't list minor involvements, jobs you held for a week, or a book you meant to read but didn't. A list of impressive activities that you know nothing about and have done nothing more than sign up for is worthless and dishonest. The student who founded the Nuclear Awareness Club in May of his junior year and now lists himself as president is clearly not so much interested in nuclear awareness as in nice-looking credentials on his application. And the less said the better about the girl who listed her two favorite books as *Canterberry* [sic] *Tales* and *Wuthering Heights* by Jane Eyre. These questions ask for simple, matter-of-fact answers about what has interested you and engaged your time; be complete, clear, and, above all, honest.

The Real Essays

If the application asks you to select *one* activity, achievement, or experience and discuss what it means to you, the question requires a response, whether short or long, that is not simply factual — it requires choice. These are the tough ones. They come in three varieties:

The "You" Question

Most of these boil down to "Tell us about yourself." Some examples:

1. A personal statement.

"Write an essay which gives the Committee on Admissions a sense of you as an individual. Suggested topics might include one of the following . . . or any personal theme that strikes your imagination" (Columbia University).

"Because other segments of this application are formally structured, we have included this form to enable you to tell us more about yourself as a person. For example, you may want to share with the Admission Office something about the experiences that have shaped your personal development, or you may want to discuss your goals, values, or ideals. We seek a response that will help us to know you better" (Princeton University).

2. Describe a significant interest or experience.

"A special interest, experience, achievement, or anything else you would like us to know about you" (Hamilton College).

"Evaluate a significant experience or achievement that has special meaning for you" (Bucknell University).

"What experience has been most significant to you personally? How has it affected your life?" (Boston University).

3. How have you grown and developed?

"Possible topics include . . . a change that you have noticed in yourself or your surroundings . . ." (Northwestern University).

"An autobiographical account" (Pace University).

The "Why Us?" Question

These questions focus on your choice of school or career as self-reflective. Some examples:

4. Why have you selected College X?

"Please discuss your reasons for pursuing a university education and explain why you want to attend BYU to attain your educational goals" (Brigham Young University).

"How do you think attending Simmons will affect your future?" (Simmons College).

5. Why have you chosen this career or profession?

"Please tell us your thoughts about your future. How do these thoughts relate to your choice of major?" (Georgetown University).

"Please describe the reasons that influenced you in selecting your intended major field of study . . ." (University of Maine).

The Creative Question

These questions give you a broad range of choices through which to reveal yourself. Some examples:

6. The national issue question.

"What do you think has been the most important social or political movement of the twentieth century? Do you share a personal identification with this cause?" (Trinity College, CT).

"Discuss some issue of personal, local, or national concern and its importance to you" (Common Application).

7. The famous person question.

"If you had an opportunity to interview any prominent person — living, deceased or fictional — whom would you choose and why?" (Boston University).

8. The hero question.

"Do you have heroes? Explain (Bowdoin College).

"Identify a person who has had a significant influence on you and describe that influence" (Wesleyan University).

"Select the Man or Woman of the past decade. Justify your selection and write about the accomplishments he or she made" (DePauw University).

9. The speech or article.

"You have been elected to speak at your high school or college graduation. What will you say? (Write your speech)" (Boston University).

"You have just been appointed editor of a major news publication. Write your first editorial" (Trinity College, CT).

10. The book question.

"What have you read that has had a specific significance to you? Explain (Bryn Mawr College and Dartmouth College).

"Your favorite or least favorite book and why" (Hamilton College).

11. The challenge question.

"Discuss the greatest challenge you have had to face or expect to face" (Dartmouth College).

12. Your high school curriculum.

"How do you think your high school's curriculum could be improved for the next generation of high school students?" (Bryn Mawr College).

13. Good advice.

"What is the best piece of advice you have ever received?" (University of Pennsylvania).

"If you were to look back on your high school years, what advice would you give to someone beginning their high school career?" (Simmons College).

14. Quotation.

"Please respond to two of the three following quotes within the space provided only: 'The things taught in schools and colleges are not an education, but the means of education.' Emerson/ 'All human actions have one or more of these seven causes: chance, nature, compulsion, habit, reason, passion, desire.' Aristotle/ 'A ship in a harbor is safe, but that is not what ships are built for.' Shedd" (Emory University).

15. The invention question.

"If you could invent anything, what would you create? Discuss" (Goucher College).

"You have just won a prize for an invention. Describe the invention and why you created it" (Vassar College).

. . . and there are others.

Underlying all these questions is choice. The question may be direct and ask you to choose something about yourself to discuss, or it may be indirect and require you to write about something either relevant or tangential to the admissions process. Some

schools ask you to explain why you chose them or why you chose college at all. Others like a less relevant go-between: choose an event, person, book, quotation, woman of the year, photograph, or invention. You may have to choose a topic; you will certainly have to choose and limit what you include in your response.

Why is the process of choice a significant source of information about the applicant? Why do so many colleges believe they will learn about you — and some think they can learn the most about you — by observing the choices you make? (Note that interviewers employ this technique, too: "If you were a color, what color would you be?" "Whom do you admire most?") First, choosing shows *preferences.* Personality assessments and tests like the Myers Briggs Type Indicator use preferences to draw conclusions about character, personality, and counseling. Are you an arts person or a hard-facts science type? Certainly, there is a difference between the person who would like to talk to Machiavelli about the cold war and someone who would share a tuna-fish sandwich with Isolde to find out what it's like to be the object of a great and doomed passion. The choice would be revealing.

Second, choice also reflects *values.* The person who drives a tomato red 1971 Volkswagen until rust leaves nothing for the floorboards to cling to is making a statement about how he wants to spend his money and what he cares about. We say, "That dress isn't me" or "I'm not a cat person." In choosing, you indicate what matters to you and how you perceive yourself.

Third, choosing shows *how* you think. Are you whimsical, a person who chooses on impulse? Or are you methodical, careful, a person who gathers background information before choosing? Questions about you and about career and college reflect these choosing patterns, and even a question about a national issue can show your particular *thinking style, level of intelligence, and insight.* The process, too, is under scrutiny here — how carefully the question has been considered, how extensive is your knowledge, how seriously you regarded the choice.

Do you analyze and think about things that happen to you? Do you feel most comfortable discussing recognized issues, writing about AIDS, South Africa, the tragedy of the space shuttle Challenger? Are you a risk taker, writing an essay that makes a case for itself out of missing socks, lunch with A. A. Milne, the heroic qualities of Antonio Salieri? Do you respond with a direct answer or go wordy and pompous: "One concept that I've been concerned with recently is reality."

The college regards your choices as a way to evaluate your preferences, values, mental processes, creativity, sense of humor, and depth of knowledge. The writing itself reflects your power of persuasion, organizational abilities, style, and mastery of standard written English. You can see why so many colleges want an essay and why admissions personnel read folder after folder. It's a very fruitful piece of the puzzle. Ten aspects in 500 words! The essay is worth your serious attention. Give it all you've got. IT MATTERS!

The Questions

The goal of all three types of questions is the same: to gather more, and more personal, pieces of the jigsaw puzzle of you for the admissions office to consider. Since the goal is the same — to get you to reveal yourself through your choice — the strategy is the same for handling what seems like, but is not, an incredible diversity of questions.

A Closer Look at the "You" Question

Many colleges ask for an essay specifically about you.

"In what ways have you grown intellectually during your years in high school?" (Amherst College).

"Evaluate a significant experience or achievement that has special meaning for you" (Common Application).

"You are strongly encouraged to use the space provided below to describe yourself, your previous academic performance and general interests" (Alfred University).

"There are limitations to what grades, scores, and recommendations can tell us about any candidate. Please use the space on the back of this page to let us know something about you that we might not learn from the rest of your application" (Yale University).

"This is your opportunity to tell us about yourself. What would you most like the Admissions Committee to know about you in reading your application" (Georgetown University).

These questions boil down to "Tell us about yourself," a query you enjoyed answering when you had to devise a yearbook quotation. You weren't intimidated then, and don't be now! The school just wants to know you better and see how you'll introduce yourself.

ADVANTAGES OF THIS QUESTION

1. It is direct. The college is asking you to add a clearer sense of you to your application. Remember, it's your best subject!
2. It is an open opportunity to speak for yourself, to plead your own case. If this is where you want to go to school, now is the time to put all you've got into letting them know that you're a "must admit" candidate. Your essay should reveal your personality, warmth, insight, and commitment.

DANGERS OF THIS QUESTION

1. It is extremely open-ended. Remember that selection is the key. Find just one or two things that will reveal your best qualities. Focus is very important. (Use the essay process described in Chapter 5 to get a good focus.)
2. There is a temptation to default and tell everything, rather than focus on a single, illuminating point. Beware of the unedited autobiography.
3. Tone: You may feel self-conscious but you don't want to sound distant and academic. Some students use their stuffiest style and forget this is a personal essay. They think they ought to sound scholarly and write essays full of sentences like:

> "Multitudinous *homo sapiens* in our contemporary culture are so engrossed in the trivia of material acquisition and success that they lose their intimate relationships with the essential elements of life: love, learning, and liberty. I myself am not one of those people."

Capitalize on the directness of this question and avoid the pitfalls. Look at yourself as a text, brainstorm and select an interpretation — one focus, one view of yourself — to send to the college. Then back it up with real and vivid events from your life that *prove* the interpretation you've chosen. Several strategies for doing this appear in Chapter 5.

Exploring the "Why Us?" Question

Some schools ask for an essay about your choice of a school or particular career.

"How do you think Middlebury College will contribute to your intellectual development and to your overall growth as an individual."

"Briefly share with us the factors which have led you to pursue an education at Bentley College."

"Please relate your interest in studying at Georgetown University to your future goals, giving any specific reason for choosing the course of studies which you have selected."

"Assess your reasons for wanting to attend college. How have your previous experiences influenced your current academic and/or career plans?" (University of Vermont).

They are looking for information about your educational direction and career goals. They also want to get an idea of how much you know about them, what research you've put into your choice process, and how serious your commitment is to this particular school.

ADVANTAGES OF THIS QUESTION

1. It is directly about you, an area in which you have great expertise.

2. You will not have difficulty finding something to write about. You have already been through the business of selecting schools and choosing X over Y; your reasons and choices are familiar and settled.
3. The focus is provided: why you chose the school. The proof is right in the catalog.
4. It is very important to understand where you're going and why. Bennington's study of successful students found that intelligence, emotional stability, and *a solid knowledge of Bennington and its philosophy* made their students succeed. Therefore, the information used in your answer is as important to you as it is to your application.

DANGERS OF THIS QUESTION

1. You might not know your subject thoroughly enough. If you've chosen New York University because you want to be close to urban night life, this says something about your academic commitment. If you're going to Smith to major in dance, the school can tell how carefully you've chosen (Smith doesn't have a dance major).
2. Again, tone can be a problem. You want to be neither arrogant nor self-effacing. Rather than trying to flatter the reader, show a concrete knowledge of the school. Bernard Ravina, a freshman at Columbia, cautions, "Don't compliment the school outrageously . . . snivelling is not good for you and it is not good for the impression you are trying to create." Nancy Donehower, assistant dean of admissions at Reed, complains, "Too many kids give us an ingratiating answer drawn from the catalog. It's insincere and it doesn't fool anybody."

Know the college and say, in a matter-of-fact way, why it is the one for you. This is your focus. Don't forget the proof, your specific and factual knowledge of the college's programs and special advantages. Name names, course offerings, professors, facilities. Make a clear and vivid connection between you and the school. Chapter 5 offers two strategies for dealing with this question.

Understanding the Creative Question

The last kind of question provides a more creative outlet for your response. Instead of trying to get a look at you through your choice of school, the colleges that use this question try to evaluate you through your choice of some tangential item: a national issue, a famous person, what you would put in a time capsule, a photograph.

"If you could travel through time and interview a prominent figure in the arts, politics, religion, or science, for example, whom would you choose and why?" (Common Application).

"Tell us about a teacher who has had a significant impact on your intellectual growth. How?" (Bowdoin College).

"Of all the books you have read, which has made the deepest impression on you? Why?" (DePauw University).

" 'Reading is to the mind what exercise is to the body.' Attributed to Sir Richard Steele, 1709. Please discuss a book you have read recently which exercised your mind and perhaps also affected your behavior" (Smith College).

"Please attach a photograph of something that has special meaning for you. Explain your choice" (Vassar College).

This, too, is an essay about you. The school is looking at your creativity and the breadth of your knowledge and education. They may find out if you read the papers, or just listen to five minutes of news when your favorite rock station takes a break. They may find out what you've read and how much you've thought about it. They may also find out if you can put yourself into an imaginary situation.

ADVANTAGES OF THESE QUESTIONS

1. A focus is provided. The range of your answer is somewhat limited by the question's designation of a hero, book, or national issue. You have something to react to.
2. The creative part of this question can help you with your proof, the evidence of the "you" that you're sending them. This is actually not such a hard question because the proof is easy to find once you've chosen your focus.
3. It can actually be fun! Your focus is you as an artist? Send a photo of your work or have lunch with Renoir. Your focus is the creative you? Send an X-ray of yourself or nominate Robin Williams as man of the year.

DANGERS OF THESE QUESTIONS

The creative element is a problem for many students. They forget everything they know about writing and stray off the path by neglecting substance or sense.

1. *The essay without substance.* Some seniors forget the importance of substantiation and write an uninformed essay. Don't write about lunch with a famous writer and get the titles of his or her novels wrong. Don't nominate Desmond Tutu as man of the year if you haven't been following the politics of South Africa. Research, as with the choice of school, can make a difference.

   In general, watch out for the national and international issues questions; it's very hard to be well informed. There's nothing wrong with an essay on South Africa or world hunger, if these are true concerns of yours. The rest of your application will support your choice. The problem is the insincere and therefore vague essay. Don't try to write "what they want to hear." Write about your real concerns; it's more revealing and a lot easier. A general and predictable piece of noble prose is a wasted effort if it lacks substance.

2. *The essay without sense.* Some seniors forget their purpose and write a crazy essay. Doubtless, truly creative essays can be very effective since popular topics are "safe" and therefore a little boring. Some admissions personnel, like Carol Lunkenheimer at Northwestern, say they would like to read "more quirky essays." Don Heider, at Franklin and Marshall, thinks, "A risk is worth it for the 'reach' school."

   Taking risks is a good idea but let common sense (and a few editors, readers, friends) be your guide. Admissions personnel may complain about too many "safe" essays, but risk essays can backfire. Vulgarity is never a good idea and eccentricity can be dangerous. Some essays have stuck in readers' minds so tenaciously that they were unable to form a balanced judgment of the applicant's strengths. A fine applicant to an Ivy League school began his essay, "I am a racist, a sexist, and a bigot." It was hard to imagine why that essay was there; it was hard to forget. His high school record was memorable; his application was rejected.

   We are not all creative souls. Few seventeen-year-olds can write like Russell Baker or S. J. Perlman. Few adults can! The eccentric essay is a real challenge and a risk; don't rush to that option too quickly. It's a gamble that could pay off . . . or bankrupt you.

Counselors may steer you away from certain topics. Remember Yale's instructions: "In the past, candidates have used this space in great variety of ways . . . there is no 'correct' way to respond to this essay request. . . ." No answer is wrong — but sloppy, general, insincere, or tasteless responses hurt. The travelog, the national or international issue, and autobiography may be problems because they are too extensive and therefore too general. But some of the best essays, the memorable and unusual ones, are about very similar, *just more focused,* topics.

Essays about your family, football team, trip to France, parents' divorce, or twin can be effective as long as they're focused and specific: a single Christmas Eve church service, a meal of boiled tongue in Grenoble, dipping ice cream on a summer job. The best essay I ever read, whose author went to Yale then to Oxford on a Rhodes scholarship and then to a Wall Street brokerage house, was about the author's experience on the football team.

The point is NO LEGITIMATE TOPIC IS WRONG! Use your head, be sincere, and treat anything you write about with specifics and focus. Chapter 5 suggests some different approaches for all of these questions.

Other Essay Problems

What if they give me only two inches in which to answer?

Some colleges, like George Washington, Bryn Mawr, Princeton, Trinity, Sweet Briar, Dartmouth, and Reed allow only a paragraph for your answer to one of these questions. Others ask for an essay on one topic and designate other topics for paragraph answers. These questions are mini-essays and should be approached with the same care and attention you gave to the Big Essay. The colleges are asking you to do the same work as other schools only to condense it all into an inch or two instead of a page or a page and a half. Use the paragraph format discussed in Chapter 3. The process, however, is the same as that described in Chapter 5. Just reduce the introduction and conclusion to a sentence each. Try to make your topic vivid in a few lines — and never sacrifice specifics.

The principle is the same, regardless of the length of your answer. You may even want to write 500 words in response to these questions and then cut to the core, to the best 100 words, so only the most direct and clearest point is left.

What kind of writing sample should I send?

Some schools require or encourage submission of an academic essay or writing sample. There is no reason not to send a school essay. As you saw in Chapter 3, a lot of college writing is similar to what is done in high school. Choose a strong performance (a B+ or better) and a paper on a not-too-esoteric topic. Do not send a 15-page term paper or a collation of library research. A short, illuminating essay on one poem, one lab experiment, one incident in history, is a good choice. Have a little consideration for your reader and send the original (if your handwriting is good), a typed copy (if it's not), or a high-quality photocopy. And try to send a paper with a fair number of teacher comments. These show how hard you've worked and how demanding your teachers have been. Poetry and creative writing are options also. But most high school seniors do not have enough writing experience to produce first-rate poetry and fiction. Unless you've won an award or received some other type of outside encouragement for your work, stick with a good expository essay of three to five pages.

Summary

There are many kinds of applications but essentially only three types of questions, all of which are meant to reveal how you choose. The key to success for all of them is to choose a clear *focus* and then *prove* your choice. If you can persuade them, you have won the day. Prove you're a creative person, prove you belong at the college to which you're applying, prove that the world needs a better mousetrap. The proof is the key.

Also, remember that although the essay should reveal information not found elsewhere in the application, it is part of a larger pattern emerging from your application. The essay about M. Lapardieu, who shaped your life and made French exciting, may not seem very original, but it will connect to straight A's in Advanced Placement French and a teacher recommendation from the head of the language department. Your choice of Georgetown and your plans for a career in nursing will be corroborated by good grades in science and work at the local hospital. An essay on the space shuttle in an application with nothing else about astrophysics or the sciences may raise more questions than it answers. It is the proof that makes a choice valid, worthwhile, insightful. Only the essays with a clear focus and specific proof convey the best *you* to the admissions committee.

5

Focusing on You

Contrasting Two Essays

Essay 1

Throughout my high school years, there have been many factors which have influenced my interests and personality. Being a well-rounded student, I have had many experiences working with people as well as with books. I have learned a great deal through these experiences.

A major influence in my life has been my family. Their love and encouragement have motivated me to expand in many areas of interest.

Another factor which has influenced me is my involvement in many activities outside of academics. Working with my peers in musicals, tennis, dance class, volunteer work and various committee and staff work, I have gained a sense of achievement and accomplishment. I have learned to work better with people, learning the value of team effort. I have gained an appreciation for the talent and hard work contributed by each and every person concerned with the project.

Working in Maine during the past few summers, I have learned much about dealing with people in a great variety of situations. My co-employees, being older than I am, also helped me to mature and accept things as they are. Furthermore, I now know more about the economic aspect of life, both business and personal.

In college, I plan to continue to live a well-rounded life, meeting and working with people from a variety of backgrounds. I expect to prepare for a profession that permits me to be closely related to children as well as adults. I want to help people. I have gotten so much out of life through the love and guidance of my family, I feel that many individuals have not been as fortunate; therefore, I would like to expand the lives of others.

I am excited about the possibility of attending [College X]. I feel that I am ready for college. I am ready to accept the challenge of the academics. I plan to give my best to [College X], knowing that [College X] will do the same for me.

This is the kind of essay admissions personnel read all day long. It is not, however, the kind of essay they remember, nor the kind that sends a "gray zone" application to the committee for reconsideration. At a highly competitive school, it's the kind of essay that might be classified D.O.A. (dead on arrival). Most important of all, this is not the kind of essay you want to write.

William Hiss, at Bates, calls these "Boy Scout" essays. They describe an ideal student — eager, involved, loyal, thrifty, reverent — but it's a general picture, not a real person. The college can't make use of this kind of picture. (In fact, in 1982, Yale changed its essay question, hoping to broaden the range of responses and reduce the number of predictable or "safe" essays they received. Vassar's photograph question was in part motivated by the same intention.) This essay does not *add* to the application because it is unfocused and too general; it could apply to any high school senior. Okay, you didn't summer in Maine. Make that California or any place in between. And you were more interested in lacrosse and the yearbook than tennis, dance, and the school musicals. Change the college's name to the school of your choice and you're all set. Three changes. Whatever else this essay has going for it, it can't do much for the author if three changes could make it yours. It wastes the opportunity to convey to the admissions committee a fresh and vital sense of the writer.

Essay 2

Someday, I hope to have a career in the biological sciences. I've always enjoyed the study of science, with its plausible explanations for the 'hows' and 'whys' of our lives. My serious interest in the area of the sciences developed in my sophomore year, during which I took Advanced Placement biology. One aspect of that course I particularly enjoyed was the final project of designing, conducting, and writing up my own experiment.

Although the work involved was time-consuming, doing the experiment allowed me to see how real scientists test hypotheses. My laboratory dealt with the effects of photoperiod and temperature on the growth of *zea mays* seedlings. Not only did I have to care for and daily alter the photoperiods of the plants, I also had to measure, every other day, the heights of 76 corn seedlings. As the labs were to be researched and prepared on a college level, I spent several hours in the library at Washington University and Meramec College, using the *Biological Abstracts* to find information on experiments similar to my own which had been written up in scientific journals. The effort required by the lab really made me appreciate the scientists who spend their lives proving or disproving theories by experimentation and research.

Ironically, the experiment was personally rewarding because my original theory was actually disproved. I hypothesized that the plants with the longest photoperiod would grow the fastest. After I concluded the lab and began analyzing the data, however, I found that the plants with a *median* photoperiod grew faster. I thought that this was very exciting; potentially routine results were given a twist.

I consider my biology experiment to be a valuable scientific experience; I was exposed to the methods and materials of *bona fide* scientists, and, in a small way, felt the excitement of discovery. That laboratory intensified my interest in science. Last year, in chemistry, I conducted more self-designed experiments, including one to test the amount of copper in copper chloride, and another to determine the amount of oxygen required for survival by a fish, a mussel, and a clam. These experiments were also worthwhile, but I still consider the *zea mays* experiment to be the most exciting lab I've ever done.

A sense of this girl — her way of looking at the world, her involvement and enthusiasm — comes across. Unless you took Advanced Placement biology, did a corn experiment, read *Biological Abstracts*, learned about scientific research, and made connections between your work in that class, other classes, and your career plans, you couldn't write this particular essay. Its strengths are its clear focus (the Advanced Placement experiment) and its specifics (the class, the 76 seedlings, *Biological Abstracts*, Meramec, copper chloride, the clam). These make it memorable and unique. According to Worth David, dean of admissions at Yale, "We want a strong and well-developed personal point of view, not an institutional response." The *focus* and *proof* are what make this essay. In Essay 1, the writer assures us that her family is supportive, that she learned a lot in Maine, and that she wants to help people. But there's no evidence of any of that. In Essay 2, the writer *shows* her points. She says she enjoyed the study of science and the 76 seedlings prove it.

Most college essays fail on one of these counts: They're either too comprehensive (no focus) or too general (no proof). Those with no focus are the autobiographies and the travelogs; those with no proof are the "Boy Scout" essays. Regardless of which essays you have to write, you want them to be personal, to be distinctively yours; to accomplish this, you must write focused and specific responses.

Prewriting: Creating a Self-Outline

Step 1: Brainstorm

Begin with YOU. As explained in Chapter 4, the questions are all attempts to learn about you. Follow the basic writing process reviewed in Chapter 3: prewrite, draft, edit. These steps are as useful for a college application essay as they are for an English paper on *Hamlet.* The text just happens to be you. So begin with you.

Start by brainstorming. Sit down with paper and pencil and fill a page with statements about yourself. List things you've done, places you've been, accomplishments you're proud of. Set a timer or a time limit and write until the page is full. Write down everything you can think of about yourself: the good, the bad, the special, the obvious, the habitual, the extraordinary. Don't consider your audience at this point. This performance is just for you.

If you have followed the plan in Chapter 1, you have plenty of time. Keep a journal for a few weeks if your brainstorming is going nowhere. Record not what you do each day but your responses and thoughts about each day's experiences. This can be a valuable source of insights and ideas about yourself. Or collect "important moment" articles and interviews from magazines and newspapers. Sports figures and celebrities often recount small but enlightening incidents in their lives in response to interviewers' questions. Or use the résumé you created for your guidance counselor and recommending teachers. You can make an activities list or résumé now if you haven't done so already. Add it all to your brainstorm sheet.

Ask yourself questions: "What are my strengths? My weaknesses?" Do a little soul-searching and be as complete as possible. Add evaluative statements like "I am a stubborn person" or "I like a challenge." Be totally honest.

Now research your topic a little. There aren't any Cliff Notes and there's nothing in the public library. But you can look over your journal, or an old scrapbook or photo album and talk to your parents, friends, employer. Gather ideas about yourself wherever you can. Ask yourself why you do the things you do — what drives you out the front door at 6 a.m. to run five miles, what keeps you up past midnight trying to build a computer program. Ask yourself: What is special about me? What kind of person am I? Under what circumstances do I learn? What interests me? What do I care about? Why is swimming, to me, more a religion than a sport? What is it like growing up in Jerome, Idaho . . . or Needham, Massachusetts . . . or Glendale, Missouri?

Try to create as complete a brainstorm as possible. Do not do this in fifteen minutes one Sunday afternoon. Begin well in advance of the drafting stage and really percolate your topic. A special fringe benefit of taking the college essay seriously is that it can be a learning experience, not just for the college, but for you, too.

Step 2: Focus

Making connections is the next step. You need to analyze your topic and divide it into some manageable pieces. As you saw in the Bruce Springsteen brainstorm in Chapter 3, grouping similar ideas and events together highlights patterns in a miscellaneous collection of information. For example, is there a series of volunteer projects? Does your love of math show up in your performance in the state math competition and in your summer job at the computer store? Ask yourself more questions to establish connections, clusters, and groups.

Now focus on three or four important strengths. Keep the unusual, the individual, the vivid. Be positive ("stubborn" isn't a great quality but "committed" is), and don't be afraid of the truth; being honest is the only way to get a fresh and sincere result.

Step 3: Prove

Remember, this is an essay. Your purpose is to persuade the readers of a particular view or interpretation of your subject. That applies as much to a paper on "Dover Beach" as to a paper on you. The first requires specific evidence from the poem. The college essay requires evidence from your life.

Organize your information into a self-outline. List personality characteristics, and under each list five or six pieces of evidence from your life, things you've been or done, that validate your point. Each characteristic is a potential focus for your essay and you need to see which ones are important, which ones you can say something about.

The evidence is crucial. If you've said you're concerned with the welfare of others but can't think of more than one proof, omit it. You're not really motivated by concern for others. You thought you *ought* to be, you thought the college would like to hear that you are. But this is an example of Worth David's "institutional response." Forget it!

Look for a potentially interesting and rich focus. As you might toy with opinions about a novel's characters, setting, or foreshadowing techniques, experiment with ideas about your own goals, interests, style. Then see what things have happened to you and what things you have done that support or illuminate these preliminary thesis statements.

Your self-outline might include items like:

1. I like to work with kids
   a. Community House
   b. my little brother
   c. babysitter and mother's helper
   d. Christmas pageant for the church
   e. career interest in child psychology

2. I like classes with student participation
   a. Mr. Stiver's class
   b. drama workshop
   c. Ms. Selman's class

3. I hate sports
   a. gym is dumb
   b. in fourth grade I never got picked for a team
   c. the field hockey jocks are weird (stupid head-bands, weird socks)
   d. I've got enough compe-tition in my life already
   e. I'm uncoordinated (falling off the parallel bars in seventh grade in front of Andrea Kaufman)

4. I always put things off until right before the deadline
   a. this essay
   b. my tenth-grade research paper
   c. getting my yearbook quote done
   d. prom table

Time for more questions. About what have you written the most? What looks interesting, different (but not unflattering)? Are there any career goals here? Motivations for college? Special personal characteristics or experiences? Working with kids might be interesting if your career and college choice are related. The preference for classes with student participation might make a good essay in applying to a college with a special tutorial program. Certainly a loathing for sports is an interesting point. But where can you go with it? Can you use it to show something positive about yourself (maybe your individuality?), something other than just eccentricity or negativity? The procrastination habit is probably not something you want to share with the college; it should be overcome, not glorified.

Again, remember there are no right answers for these questions any more than for any other essay. Admissions committees are diverse groups of individuals; there isn't one thing they want to hear. After reading 20 to 50 essays a day about the charms of University X, the evils of terrorism, and the personal commitment involved in being a doctor, most admissions staffers don't want more essays on "safe" topics. How things are in Paramus, New Jersey, or New Hope, Alabama, might be more engaging. Elizabeth DeLaHunt at Sarah Lawrence laments the self-involved and self-indulgent responses that college essay questions often elicit. "We would rather have a sense of the student's place in the world, a sense of his or her relationship — context — as a person." (Sarah Lawrence, like many colleges, continues to refine and modify its questions.)

Looking for the "right" answers is therefore pointless. And it is also counterproductive. The college essay is not an assignment to create a self. "We don't want the back lot at MGM, a created scene over a barren field. We want to see the real landscape," says Bates' Bill Hiss.

When the time comes to write, don't try to find the "right answers." And don't stare at the blank paper and despair. Stare at your self-outline. This prewriting is a good launching pad. By writing about yourself in this format, you will have a beginning and "begun is half done." Don't cheat on this step. Give it plenty of time and attention. Write to write. It will pay off when the drafting begins.

Drafting: Converting the Self-Outline into an Essay

Now consider your questions. With a self-outline, you can plan and create any of the three types of essays required. Several strategies are given for each question. Take your choice. Again, there is no one right answer, no one right essay. Just remember: FOCUS AND PROVE!

Question 1: "Tell Us About Yourself"

STRATEGY 1: A STANDARD ESSAY WITH SEVERAL WELL-PROVEN POINTS

The most conservative essay about yourself would be based on two or three of the points from your self-outline and would follow a standard introduction/body/conclusion plan. Look back at Essay 1. The writer attempted one paragraph on family, one on activities, and one on jobs. It is, in fact, a well-organized essay. There is an introduction that identifies the points to be discussed, one point for each body paragraph, and a conclusion that relates the writer to the college. But although the organization of the essay is very good, its weakness is a lack of specifics.

If you choose to write this type of essay, select two or three points from your self-outline, give a paragraph to each, and be sure you give *plenty* of evidence. Don't try to do too much: two or at most three points should do it. Either choose things not apparent from the rest of your application or "light up" some of the activities and experiences listed there. Make it vivid. The difference between general (and forgettable) and specific (and interesting) can be seen in the following first and final drafts of one paragraph from a student's essay.

EXAMPLE 1

The job I had this past summer expanded my level of maturity and provided me with exposure to a world which I had not previously experienced. It involved a combination of a job as doorman and a custodial worker in a New York apartment building. This job allowed me to break out of my shell and see the spectrum of the world as a whole. I have learned balance and adaptability. And I can empathize with the hard-working people of the so-called lower class for many of them are now my friends.

EXAMPLE 2

The job I had this past summer introduced me to physical labor and some new attitudes. I worked a forty-hour week as a doorman and custodian at the Renoir, an apartment building with 120 units on East 78th Street in Manhattan. I had a black tuxedo with a striped vest for half my day and, for the rest of the day, a paint-spattered blue and white jumpsuit that said 'Howie' on the pocket. In either outfit, I often found I was ignored by the people I helped. I got a little more acknowledgment in the tuxedo. I never got a 'Hello' but I did get a few 'Thank you's' from the people I held the door for. As the custodian, I was invisible. I could go four or five hours without hearing a single word directly addressed to me. From this job, I think I learned something about New York, about furnaces, and about the human temperament when deprived of air conditioning. But I also learned something about how our society treats people who do manual labor.

There's nothing wrong with a standard essay about yourself; just give plenty of time to building up and making specific the paragraph development that proves each of your points. Do not substitute a list of activities for support. Make a point about yourself in each paragraph and then present evidence to illuminate it, to back it up.

STRATEGY 2: LESS IS MORE

For many years, Yale suggested applicants write an essay about interests, activities, background, or aspirations; they got a lot of four-paragraph essays, with one paragraph for interests, one for activities, one for background, and one for aspirations. They changed their question to avoid this "laundry list" kind of response.

You might want to draft a standard essay (Strategy 1) and then mine it for the most interesting and important point about yourself. This is especially useful if your essay is supposed to be one paragraph or half a page. Essay 1, at the beginning of this chapter, distilled to its best and most vivid paragraph, could be very effective. The writer wanted to explain the importance of her family, but she tried to do it in only two sentences! She might have done better with an essay on just that one idea — her family's support. She could have used her page to *show* the half inch of rain that fell on her first varsity field hockey game (and on her mother and father). To this picture of soggy family devotion she might have tied her extracurricular involvement and the source of her own commitment to help others. There's a lot to be said for taking a small focus and really *showing* it to the reader.

The student who wrote about his summer job also ended up using a "less is more" strategy. He had originally begun with an essay of several paragraphs — one for clubs, one for sports, one for jobs (Example 1), and one for career plans. The final essay focused only on the summer job and tied it to several other revealing points. Drafting helped him identify the best point; other ideas were subordinated to it. He ended up with two strong paragraphs (one given in Example 2) instead of four flabby ones. (See Sample 1 in Chapter 6 for a personal essay that focuses on five minutes of dipping ice cream.)

Cleopatra had herself delivered to Antony rolled up in an Oriental carpet. I imagine it was a rather memorable delivery. The "less is more" essay makes a vivid self-presentation from within a simple (even ordinary) framework.

STRATEGY 3: THE NARRATIVE ESSAY

The most focused and narrow approach to the "Tell us about yourself" question is a short and vivid story. Omit the introduction, write one or two narrative paragraphs that grab and engage the reader's attention, then show how this little tale reveals you. Sample 3 in Chapter 6 uses something like this strategy. The writer begins with an introduction, then tells the story of a conversation from which he draws a picture of himself, his background, his insights. This type of essay puts the proof first

and the focus last. It's a little more risky but it can be very interesting. If you're a good writer, give it a try; if not, rely on a more conservative strategy.

Your procedure for the "You" question is:

1. Brainstorm yourself toward a self-outline.
2. Focus on several of your distinctive qualities.
3. Prove what you say with extensive and vivid evidence.
4. Use several proofs or a fully described incident for each body paragraph; do not write a list of activities, a travelog, or an autobiography. Avoid pure chronology.
5. Choose one of the following:
   - a standard essay with several equal focus points in several well-developed body paragraphs
   - a "less-is-more" essay that uses one experience to make several points
   - a short narrative that leads to your focus

6. *Be specific!* None of these styles of a "tell-us-about-yourself" essay will hurt you as long as you remember to make it concrete, detailed, vivid.

Question 2: "Why Did You Select College X?"

The focus and the proof for "Why Us?" questions are provided: The focus is the connection between you and the school; the proof is in the catalog. Review the pluses of the school and how you came to choose it. Find connections between the college and the points on your self-outline. Then decide what percentage of the essay ought to treat the school and what percentage ought to treat you.

STRATEGY 1: A STANDARD ESSAY ON THE SCHOOL'S PLUSES

Using the standard introduction/body/conclusion format, you can write an essay whose body paragraphs are the points about the school that are attractive to you as a prospective freshman. Do some research. Read the course catalog and viewbook carefully, and see what is offered that appeals to you. From this you can focus on the main connection between you and the school. Your body might begin with one paragraph on small points — location, climate, size, the composition of the student body — and build to one or two paragraphs on the more significant factors — curriculum offerings, class settings (tutorials, conferences, mass lectures), majors, special programs.

If you're sure of your career goal, make this your thesis; then show what the school has to offer in your particular area of concentration. Be sure they do have what you need and want. This is as important for you as it is for them. Is the faculty first rate? (Ask friends or teachers about the faculty roster.) Are there some well-known people in your field teaching there? Does the library have a unique section devoted to American political science, Judaica, the letters of Ernest Hemingway? Do some research and mention specific factors that tie in with your primary interest. For example, if you plan to concentrate in international relations, you might mention the college's Chinese language and literature program, its Junior Year Abroad option, or the short-term work-study program at the United Nations.

Avoid an ingratiating tone. Instead, *prove* whatever you say. Point out the real advantages of a particular school or program.

Georgetown's nursing program is one of the best in the nation and grants a B.S. in Health Sciences rather than just the R. N. I like the fact that graduate assistants do not teach the undergraduate courses and also the option of taking graduate courses for credit while I'm still an undergraduate. Since I would like to earn a Ph.D. in nursing and teach in a university hospital, Georgetown has the right program for me.

It's to your advantage as a potential freshman to scrutinize the place where you will live for four years, become an adult, and spend in excess of $50,000. Your answer, paragraph or essay, should show your interest and prove the school's distinctiveness in that area. It will become apparent if a school was chosen whimsically or because your boyfriend is a junior there. Dig in, find out, and then use your knowledge.

STRATEGY 2: THE SCHOOL AND YOU

Some colleges ask for an essay that connects you to them:

"Assess your reasons for wanting to attend college. How have your previous experiences influenced your current academic and/or career plans?" (University of Vermont).

This is an essay primarily about you. It asks only secondarily about your choice of college. Write a personal essay as suggested in Strategy 1 or 2 of Question 1 above. Then use the conclusion to make a connection to the college. The second type of conclusion discussed in Chapter 3, one that serves as a springboard for futher ideas, may be helpful here.

In Essay 1 on page 86 the writer set out to show the importance of her college choice in her conclusion, but there was no substance to her paragraph. See Sample 2 in Chapter 6 for similar troubles with the same question. Had she mentioned the college's preprofessional studies in law or its special 3-2 program in nursing she would have created a real connection between her plans to help others and her choice of college. Wherever you show why College X is for you, be specific and well informed.

Your procedure for the "Why Us" question is:

1. Brainstorm yourself toward a self-outline.
2. Research the college for the qualities that make it special to you.
3. Connect yourself to the college. Select one of the following:
   - Make several body paragraphs from these connections, building toward the most important ones.
   - Write an essay about yourself that comes to the *conclusion* that X is the college for you.
4. Research is the key to good proof; highlight *real* connections between you and the college.
5. Avoid an ingratiating tone. BE SPECIFIC.

Question 3: Be Creative

STRATEGY 1: BEGIN WITH YOU AND LET THAT DICTATE A CHOICE

If you have a creative question, there is again some built-in help. If you've been directed to write about a lunchmate, book, or photo, consult your self-outline and with a suitable focus select the topic that corresponds to a particular quality of yours.

If you're artistic, have lunch with Georgia O'Keefe and make your conversation with her reveal your interests in art. If you're a violin virtuoso, nominate Isaac Stern for man of the year and *show* that you know why he deserves it. You're a creative soul? Send Vassar a photo of your Grateful Dead Halloween costume. In an essay about the creation of the outfit and other similar activities, *show* them you have the imagination and skills to conceive and execute other original ideas. Harvard liked an application essay about chocolate; the writer used her job in a candy store to show her insight, judgment, and creativity.

You can use a standard essay form here. The focus is your choice. Your body paragraphs should describe the pleasures of that book, the advantages of lunch with Charles Darwin, or the three major changes you would enact at your high school. Again, remember that it is the specifics that will make or break this essay. Sample 4 in Chapter 6 fails not because the author wanted to have lunch with Monet, but because she did not know enough about him. Read up a little on your dinner guest, review that novel you've chosen, talk to your high school principal. Your initiative and sincerity will show in the specificity of your end result.

STRATEGY 2: A PRODUCTION PIECE

Shakespeare said, "the poet's pen/ Turns [things unknown] to shapes, and gives to airy nothing/ A local habitation and a name." An essay may, likewise, in a variety of ways, give a "local habitation and a name" to you. A purely creative essay can reveal your imagination, willingness to take a risk, creativity, and insight. If the question is totally without limits, an imaginative piece may demonstrate the most about you.

Worth David, dean of admissions at Yale, says, "We hope to get a sense of the person, the individual. The vehicle can be almost anything." Thus, it is almost impossible to give advice. It is helpful only to say that some students have found that a sense of themselves as individuals was most evident in an original piece — a meditation on their nickname, a speculation about elm trees, a hypothesis about socks (see Sample 5 in Chapter 6). It's risky, but for some students, it is the right risk and very effective. You're on your own with this one; good luck!

The procedure for the creative question is:

1. Brainstorm yourself toward a self-outline.
2. Choose a representative quality from the self-outline.
3. Connect this quality to a choice that will illuminate it: an artist if painting is important to you, the charms of Faulkner if you're a budding writer, and so on. Be sincere and do not try to choose "what you think they want."
4. Research your choice.
5. Write a SPECIFIC and vivid defense of your subject.
6. Get a second opinion.

Summary

A standard essay, well-organized and specific in its focus and proof, is a reasonable answer for any question. Neither predictable answers nor innovative choices make memorable essays unless you SHOW the rightness of the choice. Ronald Reagan is a better choice than Woody Allen for man of the year only if you argue it persuasively. A very good case could be made for Woody Allen, too, but only if you've got four great reasons and lots of evidence from specific films to back it up. FOCUS AND PROVE, no matter what!

The dangers are not in the topics themselves. When admissions people complain about travelogs and autobiographies, it is the lack of focus, the broad angle that is the downfall of these essays. When counselors advise students against responses about trips, sports, twins, divorces, it's because lack of proof, the generality of these essays, can be a problem. Memorable essays on any of these topics exist, by writers who took a narrow focus and backed it up with plenty of vivid specifics. Choose a strategy that feels comfortable, and be specific.

The High Risk Essay

Does the following dilemma sound familiar to you? "I'm about to apply to a school with 13,000 applicants and 1,300 places. Is it wise to aim for a big impact? I need a high-powered performance that's going to get me in!"

Keep in mind that, although the essay is important, no single aspect of the application can get you into a college. The essay can make a difference but it is not sensible to believe that a knock-out essay will get you into a school you're not generally qualified to attend. Don't try to do something that will "make up for all the rest" of your application — it will only lead to embarrassment and disappointment.

Okay, you are a qualified applicant for this school, but you need to stand out. You've decided you want to be different. You've had it with "safe" and decided you want to write an essay that is a "powerful tipper" for your case. Can it be done? Maybe.

Think of the Academy Awards. Well over a hundred people make similar acceptance speeches that night. What makes any of them stand out in our memories?

1. *Surprise* does. Some acceptance speeches say things we aren't expecting to hear. You could write about a point from your self-outline that few other writers would choose. For example, instead of writing about your concern for children, you could write about why you hate sports.

2. *Form* can do it. Some speakers surprise us not with what they say but with how they say it. A narrative essay may have enough suspense (if it isn't too long) to give this added element. The essay on a job in a candy store included a chocolate *Veritas* (Harvard's motto). It won't get an applicant accepted, but it is memorable.

3. The *unusual* can grab lagging attention. Special circumstances — and I mean really special — can make a distinctive essay. "When I first realized that my mother was deaf, it did not affect me much at all; my transactions between the deaf world and the hearing world had become a matter of course. . . ."

Supplementary materials may help here, too. The student who described a 250-toothpick bridge that supported 286 pounds and won him a physics competition made it real by sending the bridge along. But think a long time about sending support material. Send only something individual, of very high quality, and related to the total impact of your application. The toothpick bridge would not have enhanced the application if seven others were sent, if it had supported only eight pounds, or if the applicant were a music major. Research the admissions committee a little before you send anything. If faculty are involved, tapes, artwork, and projects may get more attention. But remember the volume of applications that have to be reviewed and don't expect more than your share of attention.

4. *Humor* usually works — *real* humor. A lot of high school humor is goofy, embarrassing, or in poor taste. Just remember Noel Coward's advice: "Wit ought to be a glorious treat, like caviar. Never spread it about like marmalade." Get a second (and a third) opinion.

5. And, of course, *shock* can do the job . . . either for or against you. You want to be clever not silly, a risk taker not a fool. John Bunnell, associate dean and director of freshman admissions at Stanford, cautions that, "The problem is there's a thin line between being humorous and being flip, between being creative and being eccentric. Taking risks is not a negative quality but there ought to be some common sense involved." Applicants who, given one day in time to spend with anyone in history, choose Christie Brinkley haven't thought much about their options.

You have to weigh the risk. Of course, there is often a high reward where there is a high risk. It takes something special to get a reader to say, "Hey, Alice, listen to this one!" And I am sure in the final hours of committee meetings on "gray zone" applications, no one has ever said, "Hey, wait a minute, what about that kid who wrote the essay about his *family*?"

But the predictable essay doesn't damn its author as much as a tasteless and vulgar attempt to astonish and surprise. Write about whatever makes you comfortable. Take a chance if that's your nature. You may find a like-minded individual on the committee who champions your application because of your essay. Whatever you write should be specific. And do get a couple of opinions on it; long hours at a desk can blur your sense of right versus ridiculous.

Editing

A Word About Word Processing

Computers are here to stay. First graders are hacking away at Apples and most high schools offer a variety of courses in computing, computer languages, and applications. Some colleges, like Drexel in Philadelphia and Stevens Institute of Technology in Hoboken, require students to buy their own computers when they enroll. Other schools have writing centers where students can use microcomputers and word-processing software for their writing assignments. Your high school may have such a facility.

If you have followed the time line suggested in Chapter 1 and are not working against an immediate deadline, it is worthwhile for you to get your hands on a computer, spend the 15 to 45 minutes it will take to master the basics of a word-processing program (like PFS Write, Bank Street Writer, or Volkswriter), and write your college essay on it. Brainstorming may be a lot easier with a keyboard and screen than with pencil and paper, and any assignment benefits from the revision and editing capabilities of a computer.

You will draft, redraft, and edit the college essay many times, and you may want to recycle and revise it into several versions for different colleges. The computer allows you to make modifications quickly and painlessly and then, while saving the original version of your paper, it will print a neat copy of the latest version without adding any new errors. You are more likely to write eight different essays truly tailored to each school if it's almost as easy to do as making eight copies of one essay. (And wouldn't it be nice to have a built-in spelling checker to hunt down and identify your errors?) Don't be intimidated by a machine. It is not hard to master word processing, and it is a useful tool for the college essay and for all your writing.

It is not worthwhile, however, to purchase a personal computer for one use; you may want to investigate whether some of the following places offer computer time:

- The high school writing center (or computer classroom after school)
- A relative's office
- The local college writing center (they might let you rent some time)
- A computer center that charges by the hour for use of their equipment

A few words of caution. Proofread carefully. Neatly typed pages tend to look perfect when they often are not. Read drafts several times. Sometimes the thorny problem areas signaled in handwritten drafts by multiple cross-outs and arrows fail to stand out on typed pages. Read the copy on the screen and then in a final hard copy draft before the last printout. The typographical errors of a computer often are different from the traditional errors of a typewriter; reformatting problems, incomplete deletions, and misplaced insertions are the new kinds of errors to look for.

Don't be overconfident just because you're using a fancy, expensive machine. Alas, it only does what you tell it to do. Revising your Bryn Mawr essay for Dartmouth is a poor idea if you forget to delete references to the advantages of living in the Philadelphia area. No matter how you produce your essay, proofread it carefully several times.

Handwritten essays are harder to read, so do type if possible. (If the application specifically asks, as some do, for your own

handwriting, make sure it's legible and not crammed onto the page.) I once had a student who had "dumb" handwriting. Lisa was very bright but she had big, loopy handwriting and she dotted her "i's" with cute little circles. I tried to explain to her that most people would pick up a paper like hers with a preconception that it was going to be a "C" performance at best. We finally agreed that typing her papers would free her from this subtle liability. Keep this in mind if you decide that typing takes too much time.

Editing Tips

No matter how you draft and write your essay, you will want to edit it. Remember your goal: to introduce yourself to the admissions committee. And remember your strategy: focus and prove. Reread your essay once to be sure you have zeroed in on one or two illuminating ideas about yourself and have *shown* them to your reader with plenty of specifics.

Then read the essay a second time. Look for spelling errors, sentence fragments, and confused expressions. Rewrite and revise. Some sentences cannot be improved and must be cut. When in doubt, strike it out.

Read the essay again for style.

1. Remember that good writing has a natural, easy-to-read quality. Keep the language and structure simple, direct, and clear. Don't try to hide shoddy thinking behind elaborate language. Use the fewest and simplest words possible.
2. Strike a balance between a personal and a formal tone. In a choice between a long, fancy word and a short, simple one, choose the simple word:
   a. The reason for this predicament is that the local hardware store does not have the extensive financial resources needed in order to be able to stock every size of every hardware item.
   b. Hardware stores can't afford much variety.

   a. Having been involved in theater arts activities for many years, on a wide variety of levels ranging from high school to independent repertory theater, I have naturally gained a fairly comprehensive acting experience.
   b. My knowledge of acting comes from high school productions and independent repertory theater work.

   a. I have an intense affinity for learning in a liberal arts environment that has extensive course offerings from which to choose.
   b. I want the choices that a liberal arts education offers.

   The language used in the "a" samples distances the reader, something you do not want to do in your college essay. Avoid the thesaurus, be yourself, and don't substitute a stuffy style for substance.
3. Remember that your audience is the admissions committee, not the English faculty's poet-in-residence or the chairman of the chemistry department. They are reading hundreds of applications, they are a group of individuals with individ-

ual ideas of what the college needs and wants, they are not scholars, and they are pressed for time. Be intelligent and knowledgeable, but above all, be yourself.

4. Avoid clichés and sentences that sound good but don't mean anything. For example, don't end with a line like, "I'll bring as much to College X as X will give to me." "To learn, to love, to live" sounds great — alliteration always sounds great — but it doesn't say much. Make every sentence count.
5. Avoid worn-out literary sources. Essays about *Jonathan Livingston Seagull* and *The Prophet* are pretty tired, and over-used quotations, old saws, and familiar maxims will sap the freshness of your performance.
6. Don't "sling the bull." Using words carelessly or inaccurately will only hurt your chances.
7. Use active verbs and vigorous expression. Instead of "Due to my parents' coaxing, I decided to try once more" say "My parents coaxed me to try again." Instead of "My interest in sports was encouraged by my father" say "My father encouraged my football career."
8. Avoid empty words and phrases like "really," "special," "unique," "interesting," "each and every," and "meaningful."
9. Avoid vague and predictable conclusions: "I learned a lot," "I interacted with others different from myself," "I benefited from the love and support of my family," "I learned to work with others."
10. Proofread, proofread, proofread. The essay that began, "If there is one word that can describe me, that word is 'profectionist,'" did not make a favorable impression on the admissions committee at Bates. An admissions staffer who graduated the previous June or a senior student intern may not disqualify you for grammatical errors, but why take the chance? Essays are read as an indication of writing skill. You might get the chairman of the English department as your reader!

Now put it all away for a week. Then reread it two more times for errors. Your essay doesn't have to win a Pulitzer prize but it should show both effort and commitment in its clarity, specificity, and correctness.

Make the Essay Yours

Colleges expect you to get some help with your essay. Your counselor might talk to you about choosing a subject and your parents or a teacher might help proofread a final draft. These are legitimate steps of the brainstorming and editing processes and all writers get some of this kind of help.

But only you can write your essay. The essay should introduce you to the college and no one else can speak for you but yourself.

Just as you would not use someone else's SAT scores or falsify your grades, you must not include any part of a published work or another student's writing in your college essay. This is plagiarism and, if it is discovered, your application will be denied. Your high school will be informed and all of your applications may be affected. Even if you're not caught, you have misrepresented yourself to the school. You don't want to end up at a college knowing that you got in on false pretences.

Don't let someone else write your essay for you either. Do not use a service that offers to help you with your essay "line by line, if needed," for a fee. Colleges are not the enemy anxious to find a reason to deny you admission. As a general rule, the right credentials for the right school will not be ignored. Many schools in this country accept the majority of their applicants. You and the school are in a cooperative process of "mating." Misrepresenting yourself cannot help; it's neither satisfying nor mature. If you are ready to go to college, then you are ready to accept your successes and failures as your own. Do it yourself!

Summary

No matter what questions you have to answer, begin with yourself. Brainstorm and focus on one or two points that will introduce and illuminate you to the admissions committee.

Then select your strategy. Write a short, legible, and correct essay, standard or varietal, that SHOWS the qualities about you that you have chosen to illuminate with vivid specifics, not generalities.

Revise, proofread, and type it up. Photocopy your various application packets and mail them off. Check with your recommending teachers and with the guidance office to be sure they've contributed their share. Then relax. If you've followed the time line and the steps outlined in this book, once the colleges to which you've applied have made their decisions, you will probably have the luxury of yet another opportunity to choose.

6

Analyzing Six Essays

The six sample essays that follow demonstrate a variety of strengths and weaknesses. None is presented as a perfect or "correct" college essay. Laura Fisher, director of admissions at Harvard, says the essay is "in some ways, the most important part of the application, in many ways the most personal part." Thus for admissions personnel, "there is no one standard." These samples are meant to suggest the number of options you have in introducing yourself to a college.

Sample 1

I've been told by many of my friends, teachers, and relatives that majoring in English is stupid. Whenever I tell people what I intend to do, they look at me as if I've said that I intend to major in Frisbee or creative gum chewing. These doubting Thomases invariably inform me that English majors all over the country are eating in soup kitchens and collecting welfare checks. They tell me that a liberal arts education is nothing more than a four-year escape from life, and that I should put my intelligence to some better use such as business education or chemistry. Nature, however, never geared me for these fields. Obviously, my genes have predestined me for fiscal failure.

I do, of course, have a practical side that warns me, "Susan, that's all well and good but how can you expect to get anywhere with a major in English? Let's face it, kid, the people who are warning you away from English know from experience that being a wordmonger is, at best, a risky business."

If I were like many people, my solid practical side would win out. I would dutifully throw away my complete Shakespeare and shop around for a quickie Berlitz course in COBOL. I would probably get richer quicker if I took practical courses in college and forgot about English. But I just can't compromise my belief that learning to use the English language is a timely and sensible thing to do.

My cousin, who recently graduated from Wesleyan University with a major in art, is now trying to find work as a waiter. My grandfather sees this as a prime indicator that I should go into investment banking. I, however, fail to see anything devastating about waiting on tables. In fact, one of the nicest things I ever experienced occurred when I was working at Dairy Delight.

My job as a salesperson and ice cream scooper is not particularly lucrative or challenging, but it keeps me in records and clothes. It also serves as a great opportunity to meet people. One night I was behind the counter when two men came to the window. As I poised my pencil to take their order, I was confronted with a request unlike any I had ever heard. The confused-looking man said, "My wife wants something like a dipped, almond walnut maple butter krinkle koated sugar cone. Maybe I'd better go back and ask her what she meant."

I, however, sensing a challenge, said, "Wait, I bet I know what she wants. Could it be that she wants a double scoop of butter almond and maple walnut ice cream in krinkle koat on a sugar cone?" The man breathed a sigh of relief and agreed I was probably right.

As I portioned out the ice cream, I couldn't help but think how funny the man's request had sounded. When I handed him the cone, I drawled, "Here's your super dooper double scoop of krinkle koated flipped out skipped out joy food.''

The man just grinned and said, ''Oh, that's what those things are called!'' Then he ordered a hot tin roof, hold the butterscotch. I returned with a ''*comble chaud, sans la beurre d'Ecosse.*'' My customers were suitably impressed. The second man ordered a coffee ice cream cone, and my muse rolled over and died. Returning with his order, I sighed, ''Here's your cone. I'm creatively spent!''

In all, the order took about five minutes to fill, and between the antics I can remember and sundry other ridiculous things I can't, I was almost disgustingly entertaining. When the order was finally filled, and I tried to hand the men their change, they said, ''Oh, please keep it. And thank you so much!'' As they left, I just grinned and went back to work, but that fifty-two cents meant a lot to me. It meant that somebody really enjoyed the games I was playing with words, and that even the most mundane job can be fun if it's approached in the right way. During that night, I sang the theme song from *Casablanca* with a baseball coach who thinks he's Bogie, discussed Marxism with a little old lady, and heard more than I ever wanted to know about some woman's gall bladder operation.

I have aspirations of accomplishing something far more meaningful than scooping ice cream. But if going to college for four years helps me to appreciate and manipulate the English language, then at the very least it can help me to become one of the happiest ice cream scoopers in the world.

Things To Notice About This Essay

1. It has a clear and continual *focus:* using the English language.
2. It has *proof* of her interest in language: the story of the two men and the ice cream. She is specific not only in this story, but also throughout the essay (her determination to pursue English despite others' opinions, her complete set of Shakespeare, COBOL, the gall bladder).

3. It begins with a great first line and uses the "common misperception" introduction (even though it took her three paragraphs to get going). She details the idea that language study is a waste of time and then ends paragraph three with her thesis: "learning to use the English language is a timely and sensible thing to do."
4. Her tone is personal and her style is fairly casual. The essay gives us a sense of the person, a look at her interests, values, style, and humor that her numbers and scores can't show.
5. The body of the essay is primarily narrative, but it is with a small incident, not a life history, that she proves her interest in language.
6. Her conclusion is a standard summary that connects her aspirations to her college decision. It also relates to the rest of her application, a recommendation made by an English teacher, and scores on the verbal section of the SAT.

Sample 2

From the time I was able to realize what a university was, all I heard from my mother's side of the family was about the University of Michigan and the great heritage it has. Many a Saturday afternoon my grandfather would devote to me, by sitting me down in front of the television and reminiscing about the University of Michigan while halftime occurred during a Michigan Wolverines football game. Later, as I grew older and universities took on greater meaning, my mother and uncle, both alumni of the University of Michigan, took me to see their old stamping grounds. From first sight, the university looked frightening because of its size, but with such a large school comes diversity of people and of academic and non-academic events.

In Springfield High School, non-academic clubs such as the Future Physicians and the Pylon, both of which I have belonged to for two years, give me an opportunity to see both the business world and the medical world. These two clubs have given one a greater sense of what these careers may be like. In Future Physicians, I participated in field trips to children's hospitals and also participated in two bloodbanks.

Currently I hold a job at Maas Brothers. This lets me interact with people outside my own immediate environment. I meet different kinds of people, in different moods, with different attitudes, and with different values. This job teaches me to be patient with people, to have responsibility, and to appreciate people for what they are.

In the community I am active in my church Youth Group. As a high school sophomore, I was our church's representative to the Diocesan Youth Fellowship. I helped organize youth group events, the largest being "The Bishop's Ball," a state-wide event for 300 young people. I also played high school junior varsity soccer for two years. As a senior I will be playing varsity soccer, but in the off-season. As a junior I coached a girls' soccer team for the town. This gave me a great deal of responsibility, because the care of twenty-four girls was put into my custody. It felt very satisfying to pass on the knowledge of soccer to another generation. The girls played teams from other parts of Florida. Though their record was 3-8, the girls enjoyed their season. This is what I taught them was the greatest joy of soccer.

The past three years of my life have given me greater visions of my future. I see the University of Michigan as holding a large book with many unread chapters and myself as an eager child who has just learned to read. I intend to read and probe into all the chapters. The University of Michigan offers me more than the great reputation of this fine school, but a large student body with diverse likes and dislikes, and many activities, both academic and non-academic, to participate in. With the help of the University of Michigan, I will be successful after college and be able to make a name and place for myself in our society.

Things To Notice About This Essay

1. It follows a general essay organization, with an introduction, several body paragraphs about different activities, and a conclusion that returns to the earlier idea of Michigan's diversity.

2. It has no focus but rather jumps around from the school to the writer and from point to point. Notice especially the lack of transition from the first paragraph to the second: how did we get from Michigan's diversity to the writer's clubs?
3. The body paragraphs lack *proof*: what are these clubs and jobs, what did he do in each one, how many field trips were taken, and what was his role?
4. What's Pylon? What does he do at Maas Brothers?
5. There are plenty of generalizations but no evidence to back up any of them. How did these activities give him a greater sense of the career world? "Participated" and "interact" are pretty vague words. Compare the discussion of Maas Brothers with the ice cream scooper's story.
6. There is very little specific knowledge of what the University of Michigan has to offer.
7. The style is rather stuffy and awkward ("while halftime occurred," "the care of twenty-four girls was put into my custody").
8. Most important, nearly everything described here appears elsewhere on the application, under sports, jobs, extracurricular activities, and alumni connections.
9. The writer would be well advised to focus on *one* of the things discussed in this essay. Perhaps he could show the reader his work with the girls' soccer team. What he did to make Jennifer and Gretchen and Courtney enjoy soccer even though they only won three of their games would be more focused and vivid than a lot of talk about passing things on to future generations.
10. In short, the essay seems full of information and displays adequate form, but it lacks *focus* and *proof*.

Sample 3

My most important experience sought me out. It happened to me; I didn't cause it.

My preferred companions are books or music or pen and paper. I have only a small circle of close friends, few of whom get along together. They could easily be counted "misfits." To be plain, I found it quite easy to doubt my ability to have any sort of "close relationship."

After the closing festivities of Andover Summer School this past summer, on the night before we were scheduled to leave, a girl I had met during the program's course approached me. She came to my room and sat down on my bed and announced that she was debating with herself whether she wanted me to become her boyfriend. She wanted my reaction, my opinion.

I was startled, to say the least, and frightened. I instantly said, "No." I told her I on no account wanted this and that I would reject any gestures she made towards starting a relationship. I would ignore her entirely, if need be. I explained that I was a coward. I wanted nothing whatsoever to do with a relationship. I talked a lot and very fast.

To my surprise, she did not leave instantly. Instead, she hugged her knees and rocked back and forth on my bed. I watched her from across the room. She rocked, and I watched. Doubts crept up on me. Opportunity had knocked and the door was still locked. It might soon depart.

"I lied," I said. "I was afraid of what might happen if we became involved. But it's better to take the chance than to be afraid."

She told me she knew I had lied. I had made her realize, though, how much she actually wanted me to be her boyfriend. We decided to keep up a relationship after Andover.

Even then, I was not sure which had been the lie. Now I think that everything I said may have been true when I said it. But I'm still not sure.

I learned, that night, that I could be close to someone. I also realize, now, that it doesn't matter whether or not that person is a misfit; the only important thing is the feeling, the closeness, the connection. As long as there is something between two people — friendship, love, shared interests, whatever else — it is a sign that there can be some reconciliation with fear, some "fit" for misfits. And it shows that fear need not always win, that we can grow and change, and even have second chances.

I am still seeing her.

Things To Notice About This Essay

1. It follows the standard essay pattern: an introduction (short), a series of supporting paragraphs for the body, a conclusion (here, two paragraphs, a summary paragraph and an end sentence).
2. It has a *focus*: his anxiety about relationships.
3. It has *proof*: the story of his conversation with a girl. Again, focused narrative development has made the proof vivid.
4. It is short, to the point, simple, and yet memorable. It is interesting without being grand, noble, or cosmic.
5. The style is simple and direct, employing short sentences and simple words to tell a simple story.
6. It coordinates and enriches an application full of academic achievements and high scores and grades. It is definitely not something found elsewhere in the application.

Sample 4

Claude Monet, an impressionist painter, challenged the traditional ideas of nineteenth-century art. He was an individual who had the courage to follow his convictions and, as a result, was not accepted by the critics of his time.

Had Monet lived in New York City in the early twentieth century, he might have enjoyed the ambiance of Greenwich Village, a place similar to the Left Bank of Paris. The Village offers young artists a creative environment in which they can meet and exchange ideas. I would invite Monet to share a bottle of Chablis at a nearby sidewalk café.

Due to the fact the Salon never accepted Monet's paintings, he never sold any. Monet was not discouraged by their disapproval. He suggested to a few of his contemporaries to set up their own show in opposition to the Salon. This exhibit was not well received by the critics; however, a few people actually responded favorably to these innovative paintings. Shortly thereafter, Monet developed a following that appreciated his art.

One of the questions I would ask Monet was how he found

the courage to challenge the established standards mandated by the Salon. He expressed his belief that his artistic expression was acceptable. He was willing to defend his style despite the consequences. Monet's response would help me realize that if you believe in something strongly enough, you must have the faith to defend it.

Claude Monet was a man who was able to stand up for his beliefs and act upon his convictions. I hope if I were ever confronted with a similar situation, I would be able to draw upon the same courage Monet did and stand by my beliefs.

Things To Notice About This Essay

1. It follows proper essay form, although it takes two paragraphs out of five (too great a percentage) to introduce the idea of lunch with Monet.
2. It has a *focus*: lunch with Monet would be a chance to discuss standing by one's convictions.
3. It lacks *proof*: only brief and vague mention is made of what Monet suffered for his convictions. Two short paragraphs are meant to do all the work. Little knowledge of Impressionism, Monet's life, or art in France in the 1870s is revealed. For example, Monet sold many paintings during his lifetime; the writer doesn't know her subject well enough. She may have chosen this topic for the impression she hoped it would create rather than because of her interest in Monet.
4. The admissions committee looks for a connection between the essay and the rest of the application. Only a very slim connection is made here to the writer herself; she does not present herself as an art major or as a rebel. Therefore, the essay fails to support the rest of the application.

Sample 5

It has come to my attention that our nation, and nations like ours, have long been plagued by a mysterious occurrence. An occurrence that is as perplexing as it is frustrating, and as baffling as it is widespread, a problem that finds its origins at the very foot of our society. The problem of which I speak is none other than "The Orphan Sock Enigma"; the constant disappearance of individual socks during the laundering process. It is a problem familiar to all of us, and also one to which we have unwillingly admitted defeet [sic].

I recently decided that this puzzle had remained unsolved for too long, and resolved to find an explanation. (In the grand tradition of science, I refused to be discouraged by the basic irrelevance of my cause.) But the truth that I uncovered is more shocking and fantastic than I could have ever imagined. My procedures, observations, and conclusions are as follows:

First, to verify that the problem exists, experimental and control loads of laundry were completely processed (put through the washer and dryer). In the experimental load (load with socks), by the end of the process, some socks were lost. But in the control load (load without socks), no socks were lost. Thus, the problem was verified.

Next the progress of a load of socks was carefully monitored. The results indicated that sock disappearance occurs during the period of time when the load is in the dryer. Following this conclusion, a literature search was done and a very significant fact was uncovered: there is no mention of socks disappearing in dryers before the invention of dryers in the 1920s. All evidence clearly pointed to the dryer. And it is there that I would find the answer to the enigma.

Then, the actual experiment was done. In four separate trials, a number of socks (ten socks, or five pairs) were put through a normal drying cycle. The types of socks tested were selected by the highly accurate Harvey-Allman Principle Hierarchy and Zero Alternative Reduction Dimension (HAP-HAZARD).

The mass of the total load was measured prior to processing. Upon completion of the cycle, the mass of the remaining load plus the lint collected was also measured. In addition, the temperature of a running, empty dryer was measured, as was the temperature of a running, full dryer during the cycle. A table of data follows.

In each and every trial, one or two of the socks were lost (each from a different pair). More importantly, in each and every trial, there was a net loss of mass and also a net

	TRIAL #			
	#1	#2	#3	#4
Initial Mass 10 socks	265g	270g	276g	261g
Final Mass remaining socks and lint	261g	266g	271g	256g
Temp. running, empty dryer	65.56°C	65.56°C	65.56°C	65.56°C
Temp. running, dryer with socks	70.56°C	70.56°C	71.56°C	71.56°C
Net change in mass	4.0g	4.0g	5.0g	5.0g
Net change in temp.	5.0°C	5.0°C	6.25°C	6.25°C

Mass and temperature data for trials 1-4.

increase in temperature. These results suggested a test hypothesis. Through the use of Einstein's equation for mass-energy equivalence, $E = mc^2$, the net loss of mass was completely and totally accounted for by the net increase in temperature. All the evidence clearly pointed to one unavoidable, momentous conclusion: all the socks that had been disappearing in countries all over the world had been directly converted to energy (or that there was something seriously wrong with my dryer). I have just begun to realize the monumental importance and far-reaching implications of my discovery. Quite possibly, it could completely change the way we live our lives (and do our laundry) for years to come.

From further experimentation, it seems that the amount of energy liberated (and mass lost) is directly related to the amount of the fiber Spandex in the sock.

But for some reason, the Spandex must be in the form of a sock for the reaction to take place. Therefore, by increasing the amount of Spandex in a sock, one can increase the amount of energy liberated. It also seems that the reaction can be controlled by the presence of different numbers of fabric softening sheets, similar to the effect of control rods in a nuclear reactor. In light of these discoveries, my house is now completely powered by a "Sock Reactor."

I estimate that just a few "Sock Reactors" could supply

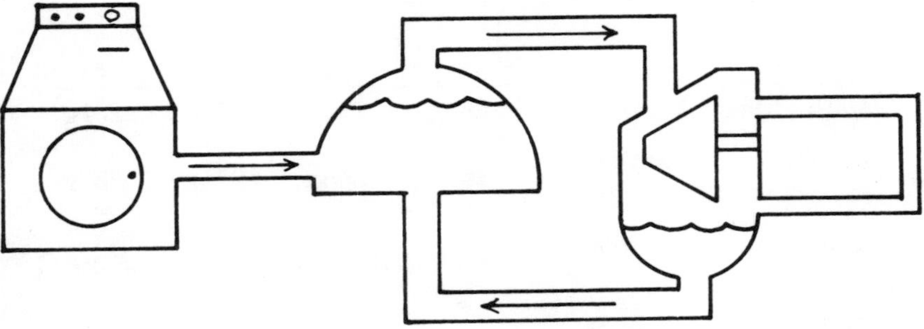

Fig. 1. Simplified Diagram of a "Sock Reactor."

power to a city the size of Chicago with zero danger (provided a good supply of fabric softening sheets are on hand). This is because one hundred percent of the mass is completely converted into energy safely, easily, and without leaving any of that unsightly radioactive waste common to those other name brand reactors. Therefore, you and your loved ones are spared from that embarrassing radiation sickness and unpleasant aftertaste.

Originally, I had hoped to keep knowledge of this discovery fairly restricted, but I fear that word has leaked out. I have reason to believe there is a merger planned between Interwoven Hosiery and General Power nuclear division.

Although I have not been able to explain why only one sock out of a pair can be converted, it appears to in some way relate to a black hole, a time warp, and static cling.

Albert Einstein, the man who first discovered the mass-energy equivalence, never wore socks. I think that just about says it all.

Things To Notice About This Essay

1. It's written in essay form. It has an introduction, several paragraphs of proof, and a clear conclusion. However, it's also a creative piece that is not easily translatable into formulas or patterns.

2. It has a *focus*: the "Orphan Sock Enigma."
3. It is specific: the problem, the research, the chart and figure make it real and vivid.
4. This is a production piece that few seniors could do. However, if you can write with comparable flair and humor, it is a reasonable option for a college essay. It presents a good picture of the writer, his interest in science, his imagination and humor, how extensively he thinks about life, and how well he can write.

Sample 6

As a member of the Wesleyan community, I can contribute extensively both in and out of the classroom. As a student I am motivated to explore as many perspectives of as many different disciplines as I possibly can. I am fascinated by the creative potential of the human mind as well as by the complexities of the universe. I enjoy the challenge of expanding my store of knowledge and experiences, and the feeling of accomplishment when I have met the challenge successfully. This attitude enables me to be an active force in the classroom, continually questioning and discovering new parallels between diverse ideas.

My enthusiasm to discover extends beyond studying specific fields of knowledge to the experience of living. I like to be surrounded by people with a variety of backgrounds and interests. I am intrigued by their differences, and make an effort to be accepting of these differences. As a result, I feel that I may be able to pull together students with different points of view. Interpersonal relationships are very important to me. I believe that communication and responsibility are the two most important elements in all human relationships. I value honesty, integrity and frankness as well as sensitivity and empathy for other people and hope to receive the same respect in turn.

It is very important for me to devote some of my time to helping others. During college I intend to continue to take an active role in social action programs. In addition to serving the community at large, I feel a personal responsibility to take an equally active role in creating a better environment for myself and others. I plan to be involved in student government and other organizations that work to this end. I hope that my personal commitment enourages the commitment to attempt productive social change.

Things To Notice About This Essay

1. It does not use a standard essay form. Since there is no real body here, the first paragraph cannot be said to introduce, nor the last to conclude. In fact, all three paragraphs are pretty much interchangeable.
2. There is a *focus*: what the writer has to offer Wesleyan.
3. There is no *proof*. There are no specifics about either the writer or the school.
4. It is full of clichés, generalizations, and lofty language and it could apply to nearly any high school senior. It does not add to the application; it is truly forgettable.
5. It does not show a strong effort to go beyond the surface aspects of the topic. It is general and therefore reveals almost nothing about the writer.

I do not recommend any of these essays to you as models. I present the six as examples of the strengths (focus, proof, simple language, structure, vividness) and weaknesses that have been discussed throughout this book. It is irrelevant what schools these essays were written for or whether the applicants were accepted. But as an important part of the overall performance and impression of an application, your essay matters. A look at these samples may help you avoid the pitfalls, enjoy the variety, and end up with an essay that gives a connected, strong, and vivid picture of you to the colleges of your choice.

Suggested Reading

Writing Skills

Barnet, Sylvan. *A Short Guide to Writing About Literature.* Boston: Little Brown and Co., 1979.

Gibaldi, Joseph and Walter S. Achtert. *MLA Handbook for Writers of Research Papers.* 2d ed. New York: Modern Language Association of America, 1984.

Murray, Donald M. *A Writer Teaches Writing.* 2d ed. Boston: Houghton Mifflin Co., 1984.

Strunk, William, Jr., and E. B. White. *The Elements of Style.* 3d ed. New York: Macmillan Publishing Co., 1979.

Sullivan, Jenny N. *Writing Themes About Literature: A Guide to Accompany The Norton Introduction to Literature.* New York: W. W. Norton and Co., 1983.

Weidenborner, Stephen and Domenick Caruso. *Writing Research Papers: A Guide to the Process.* New York: W. W. Norton and Co., 1982.

Preparation for College: From the College Board

College Board. *The College Board Achievement Tests: 14 Tests in 13 Subjects*. New York: College Entrance Examination Board, 1983.

College Board. *The College Cost Book: 1986-87*. 7th ed. New York: College Entrance Examination Board, 1986.

College Board. *The College Handbook: 1986-87*. 24th ed. New York: College Entrance Examination Board, 1986.

College Board. *Index of Majors: 1986-87*. 9th ed. New York: College Entrance Examination Board, 1986.

College Board. *10 SATs*. 2d ed. New York: College Entrance Examination Board, 1986.

Gelband, Scott, Catherine Kubale, and Eric Schorr. *Your College Application*. New York: College Entrance Examination Board, 1986.

Mitchell, Joyce Slayton. *College to Career: The Guide to Job Opportunities*. New York: College Entrance Examination Board, 1986.

Index